THE SOUL'S QUEST FOR WHOLENESS

When we think of healing we should think of wholeness; when we are seeking healing, we should be seeking wholeness.

As we reflect on our condition, we find that we are not whole—none of us is whole. If we seem to be well physically, we may not be completely well mentally or emotionally. We are not whole as a people, as a nation, or as a world. Whether our diseases be of body, of mind, of family, of finances, of work, of worth, or of fulfillment, there is always a perceived lack of wholeness of the soul that stands behind all disorders. It is the sickness of the soul which is the true reality, and our diseases and disorders are only symptomatic manifestations of it.

—from *Reflections on the Path*

Reflections on the Path

Based on the Edgar Cayce Readings

Herbert B. Puryear, Ph.D.

BANTAM BOOKS

TORONTO · NEW YORK · LONDON · SYDNEY · AUCKLAND

This book is dedicated to the Lubbock Puryears, from whom I am learning so much about the basic qualities of character in the Christian life:

William Seymour
Jettie Lou
Lela Deborah
Effie Catherine

This low-priced Bantam Book has been completely reset in a type face designed for easy reading, and was printed from new plates. It contains the complete text of the original hard-cover edition.
NOT ONE WORD HAS BEEN OMITTED.

REFLECTIONS ON THE PATH

A Bantam Book/published by arrangemet with A.R.E. Press

PRINTING HISTORY
*A.R.E. Press edition published September 1979
Bantam edition/April 1986*

ISBN 0-553-25659-9

Published simultaneously in the United States and Canada

Contents

An Invitation

You are a sojourner on your way. We do not want to detain you nor turn you from your proper course. But now that you are passing by this post, warm yourself here for a while, sup with us, rest and gain strength for tomorrow's journey, and let us talk of our experiences on the path. It is always good to see the WAY through different eyes.

We do not always talk around this campfire. Sometimes we sing and dance with joy; sometimes we listen observantly to the life about us; sometimes we gaze silently at distant horizons; and sometimes we sit motionless in quiet inner absorption.

There is shelter here. You are welcome to come and to go. We may not be here tomorrow—we are on the path ourselves, you know! The dawn of a new day draws near. Let us with the first light of the morning sun remember who we are and the path to which we are called.

Foreword

It has been my privilege since 1959 to talk with thousands of people about the Edgar Cayce readings. Following many of these presentations, some individuals have asked if it were possible to obtain a copy of the lecture. These requests have encouraged me to act on a friend's suggestion that I incorporate several of these extemporaneous talks into a book.

The purposes of a lecture, or a published collection of lectures, are different from those of the usual book with its focused development of a central theme. It has not been my purpose to theorize or speculate. Nor have I tried to develop tightly logical or scholarly articles. It is my interest, rather, to offer a different perspective and point of view, to invite further thinking and to encourage a deeper inquiry into the meaning of the phenomena and processes of life. My intent is not so much to explain as to engender a sense that life and its phenomena are explainable. It is my hope that the student will not ask whether I am right or wrong but will rather be stimulated to "search the scriptures" more deeply than ever before. By this phrase, I am referring to the Bible, of course, but also to the Edgar Cayce readings, which are indeed so worthy of deeper study. More important than what is printed on the page is the quickening of consciousness in the reader. It has been said that the work of the readings was for the seeker. If these articles encourage the seeker to continue his quest with more zeal and assurance, they will have served their purpose.

The specific stimulus to its completion in the present form is due to the continuing encouragement and indefatigable work of Kiiri Tamm, who rewrote the transcripts into second-draft form and typed and retyped the chapters. I am also very appreciative of the work and patience of Ken Skidmore and his editorial staff.

Herbert Bruce Puryear, Ph.D.

Learning to Love

What if God took you into partnership and your work with Him included the ability to endow people with omniscience and omnipotence, all knowledge and all power? What would you use as the criteria for dispensing such gifts? You might ask, "Why would God want to do such a thing?" The Edgar Cayce readings say that God created us as souls to be co-creators with Him. He wants us to choose to be companions with Him, to be free to move through all dimensions and to manifest His energy in creative expression. We speak of eight dimensions in this solar system. There may be hundreds or thousands. And we are invited to be co-creators with Him. Eye has not seen nor ear heard nor mind imagined what He has prepared for us.

What, then, if you could endow someone with infinite knowledge and power? What would be the criteria of evaluation for making such decisions? As overwhelming or even frightening as such an idea may seem, there is a very simple and satisfying answer. If you could be sure that a person would use the energy and information *always* in a fully loving way, in a selfless, helpful way, there would be no problem. I have dramatized this proposition in order to ask, "Isn't learning how to love the only thing we have to do?" God is the source of all *knowledge* and *power* and He is eager to give these to us as we demonstrate that we can be faithful (100%) stewards of them. He who is faithful over a little, will be given charge over much. That is the spiritual law of stewardship according to the Bible. The Edgar Cayce readings speak of reincarnation, karma, meditation, dreams, Atlantis, earth changes, castor oil packs, colonics and dietary changes. None of these reveals what this work is truly about.

The motto for this work, given in the readings, is "That we may make manifest our love for God and man." (254-51) That is the purpose of this work. We may think of this motto as an application of the great commandment to love God with all our hearts and our neighbor as ourselves.

We have been taught that love is *the way*, but not everyone agrees to this principle. I was leading a Sunday School discussion group and all of us were voicing platitudes about love. One sincere man said, "It won't work. It doesn't work." He was expressing more accurately than the rest of us the way we live our lives. We knew that in a Christian-oriented Sunday School class we ought to say, "Yes, of course, love is the way." But this man was a lawyer working in the state court system, and he was seeing people day after day who were in serious trouble. He said, "It doesn't work. It's not going to work and don't count on it working." Few of us believe or act that way anyway, do we? Do we really live our lives according to the kind of love that says if a man strikes you on the cheek, you turn the other cheek? How long has it been since you did that? Or if a man asks you to go a mile, you go two with him. Or if he asks for the coat off your back, you give him your cloak also.

Even if our words say that love is the way, our feelings still give us some problems. A woman who received a Cayce reading was told that she had lived during the time of Jesus and had known Him. She also had known the Apostle Peter, and had favored Peter's way. His zeal, power and action-oriented enthusiasm was more appealing to her than the serenity of Jesus' style of love. The reading indicated she felt disappointed in Jesus.

One of the most overquoted passages in the Bible describes Jesus driving the money-changers out of the Temple. We are still looking for a way of saying that He really did get angry and He truly was forceful. So we keep talking about Jesus driving the money-changers out of the Temple. Why? Because we do not truly believe that love is the way. What is the way? Protest? Politics? Science? Economics? The flower-power generation of just a few years ago said that love was the way. But were they not more militant than loving?

The readings say that Jesus could have ruled the world without raising a hand; yet He chose the way of love. The temptations in the wilderness were times when He was considering how to accomplish the work before Him. It occurred to Him, "I can go about as a psychic and a healer and everything I touch can be healed, or I can be a magician producing bread." He could have done it all, yet He chose the way of love. Do we really agree that love is the Way? When I speak of the Way, let me add a word of caution. We are so "salvation" oriented with respect to Jesus being the Way, that we are inclined to think this means He is the way *to heaven*. The Way does not refer to goals or ends but rather to how to live, the spirit or the purpose in which to do what we are doing. When you think of the Way, do not think of the way *out*. Think of the Way as the spirit or attitude in which we should do whatever is at hand. The way to do what we are doing is selflessly, lovingly and in a spirit of sharing.

Though it is universally difficult to discuss love meaningfully without seeming trite there is not one of us who does not feel that he has a certain right or need to be loved. Furthermore, most of us feel that we are never loved enough. Our parents never really loved us enough. Our spouse does not really love or care enough. Our children do not love us as much as they should. Isn't that the way we feel some of the time, or most of the time?

Even so, there is a paradox in the way we feel about our love for other people and our expectation of other people's love for us. From our point of view, the question is, "Why can't they love me the way I am? If they really loved me, they wouldn't ask me to change, they wouldn't ask me to be someone else. They would accept me for what I am." On the other hand, our feeling about others is: "If he really loved me, he would change." "If she really loved me, she wouldn't do that kind of thing." So, love to us means that everyone else should love us the way we are without requiring any change in us; and they should also change in the ways that we want them to change and they should do what we expect them to do. Such feelings about love are almost universal. But is this selfless? Is it sharing?

Consider what goes on in the name of love. Jealousy! The readings say that jealousy is one of the most destructive of all emotions. Aggressiveness! Over 60% of the murders in this country are committed within the immediate family. We kill the people we love because they are killing us. Worry! A great deal of worry goes under the disguise of love. Much of the concern expressed in this way is far more destructive than loving. Some of it can rightly be called "smother love."

We are aware of the great commandment to love God with all our hearts and our neighbors as ourselves. Yet, even if we acknowledge that we think that this is the way to be, we do not know how to go about it. We know that we *should* love; we've heard from the Gospel, "Believe, and ye shall be saved!" Yet we go about saying things like, "I just cannot love that person. I really cannot understand that person. I know it is not right, but that person is just too difficult for me." We confess to our own limitations as an excuse not to change. We do not know how to change. The church and modern psychology have been of very little help in showing us *how* to love.

Let us go back to the first commandment for a moment and consider its parts. First we are commanded to love God with all our heart, mind and soul. What does that mean? Have we ever given it any thought? When I ask people how we should love God, I almost invariably receive answers relating to love of fellow man. Yet this part of the commandment precedes love of neighbor and requires a differentiation between these. We hurry over this first part, perhaps because we have an unclear notion about what God is.

We have misgivings about the nature of God and often do not enjoy talking about what He means to us. We are afraid such talk will not be fruitful and many times it is not. What do we mean when we say we believe in God? The readings say that God means good. Can we say we believe in good? A lot of people think of the One Force in the universe as being a neutral force. Is the One Force a good force, and not a neutral one? If we thought it were, our attitude about all of life would be quite different. If we had a deep sense that believing in God meant believing in good, that the One and only Force that is operating in the universe has goodness as its intrinsic quality, then we would get a sense that goodness may come out of many things. Yet we are afraid that life will not turn out well.

Remember the writer in the New Testament who said he was persuaded that nothing can separate us from the love of God and that all things work for good for them that love God. All things work for good for those that love good, if it is indeed good that we want. The great New Testament passage in Corinthians 13 says that love does not rejoice in iniquity. Do we rejoice in iniquity? Probably more so than we imagine. Do we not rejoice sometimes when people get their due?

When a moment of judgment comes to us, we want to be forgiven. When it comes to another person, we may say he had it coming to him. He is meeting himself. So, we do rejoice sometimes when people meet themselves. Do we not get a good feeling when we see someone receiving his just deserts for something he had been bringing on himself? And don't we sometimes enjoy saying, "I told you so"? Perhaps we even pride ourselves in not saying it aloud, but we feel, "I told you so. I knew it would catch up with you!" We rejoice in iniquity. This is just one of many possible ways in which we may be failing to recognize our own unloving responses.

The readings' approach to the nature of God raises one of the most difficult theological problems relating to the modern church. When it comes right down to it, this information asserts a bigger, more beautiful and more inclusive concept of the nature of God than most of us hold.

Contemporary Christian theology differentiates strongly between God as Creator and man as the created and thus the creature. This does not seem consistent with the Biblical teachings that God is our Father and we are His children invited to be joint heirs with the Son. The readings speak of the Oneness of all force. The Bible teaches, "The Lord thy God is One." The premise of the One Force implies that everything that is is a manifestation of God. If there is only one force and it is of God, then a spark of electricity is the energy of God in motion. This insight softens the separation between Creator and created. We speak of God at work in nature and we sense Him working in the miracle of the manifest universe; but do we truly experience His presence all about us?

If we say we believe in God as omnipotent, omnipresent and omniscient, then we should sense that He is, inclusively, all there is. Let us borrow an idea from modern math called set theory. Now set theory is just a way of categorizing things, allowing for overlapping. We may say there are two kinds of people, men and women. These are discrete and not overlapping sets; but if we speak simply of persons, then "persons" becomes a set that is inclusive of the other two sets. We speak of things as being either mineral, vegetable or animal. These are three sets which are inclusive of everything manifest. The manifest universe is a set which is inclusive of mineral, vegetable and animal. The manifest and the nonmanifest constitute two sets. What would be inclusive of these two sets? Let us imagine an all-inclusive set, outside of which there is nothing else. This would be a set that includes all that is immanent and all that is transcendent. It would contain within it everything that is in any dimension—wholeness—the fullness of being. Now that all-inclusive set is my understanding of God.

God said, "I Am." He is the *ISness* of all that is. There is none other and nothing else. This is my understanding of the approach of the readings to the nature of God. Some critics of this point of view will call it pantheistic, meaning that God is in insects and birds and such as that. It is not that when we see a bird, we say, "That is God," but we should sense that the bird is truly a manifestation of God, for not one falls without His cognizance of it.

If we agree that the all-inclusive set is God and if we agree that God is good, then when we say, "I believe in God," we are affirming an *attitude* about being in reality. We are saying that we know that the Force that is at work in all the dimensions of the universe is *love*. Such an affirmation should help us change our attitudes about the meaning of life, our relationships with other people, and the things that transpire in our lives. It should transform our attitudes toward things that seem to be negative, detrimental or painful.

The undeniable reality of evil does not mean that there is an evil force in any ultimate sense. God's children, given free will and access to the One Force, make choices which are out of accord. But the force itself is good. It is of God; it is God. This attitude should give us a new approach to the universe, an integrative attitude about it, a sense of its wholeness, balance and rightness. It would be a supremely ecological attitude that would give us a sense of rightness about processes in the earth. Part of loving God is loving nature and thus the laws of nature.

The interdependence of all life in the earth plane is one of the great lessons of nature. Some believe that if everything were right in the world, then big animals would not eat little animals. It has never been clear to me why it would be better for a bird to eat a seed which might develop into a tree than to eat an insect which might destroy a tree. Love of the laws of nature presents some real and serious challenges to most of us in our present way of thinking. Can we get a sense of the beauty of the cycles of life? In the earth plane, the life cycle includes birth, growth, maturity, fruition, decline, death and decay. If we are going to say we love God and

His manifestations in the earth plane, we need to look at nature about us and get a sense of the way He works in nature. Then we must discover some way in which to learn to love those laws especially as they apply to ourselves.

Another way of saying, "I love God," would be to say, "I love natural law." Do we really love the natural law of the way our bodies work? If we know that the attempt to assimilate fried foods causes disturbances in the electrical forces of the body, do we love such principles of physiology? Do we really love the way the physiology of the body works in terms of natural law? It is amazing how magnificent the human body is with respect to movement and activity and how joyous we can feel in activity, such as a walk on the beach. Yet, we spend so little time in the open air even in the absence of good excuses for not getting out. Regular walking does marvelous things for the human body in terms of its balance, health and energy. If we do not engage in regular activity of the body, then can we say that we love the laws behind its natural functioning which require activity?

Do we love the principles of cycles? Do we love day and night and winter and summer and spring and fall? And birth and decay? The Hindus have worshipers of Krishna, Lord of Life, and of Shiva, the Destroyer. Well, they say, what if there were *only* life? What if all the cows and flies and people that were ever born never died? Someone once estimated that, if a single paramecium were allowed in an unlimited way to reproduce at its optimum rate, within five years paramecia would fill all the known universe. One of the characteristics of the earth plane is the cycle of life and death, and we do not love that cycle. In His love for us, He brings change into our lives. We may not always experience this change as pleasant, but it is always for our growth.

You have heard it said, "Love the sinner and hate the sin." I find some extraordinary things in the readings regarding attitudes toward difficult situations. A 42-year-old woman was told that until she could see the

beauty of the Creator in the vilest of the vile that she
would understand little of the relationships of the souls
of men with God and with the universe. In jealousy and
in murder, we need to be able to realize that that same
energy, that same drive, that same motivation that
destroyed had behind it a quality of the beauty of the
Creator. We need to learn a lot about love to come to
that point of awareness and understanding.

Another reading states, "How far is the vilest of
the passions of man from the love of God? Just under."
And another: ✔

**Which is the more real, the love manifested in the
Son, the Savior, for His brethren, or the essence of
love that may be seen even in the vilest of passion?
They are one. But that they bring into being in a
materialized form is what elements of the one source
have been combined to produce a materialization.
Beautiful, isn't it?**

**How far, then, is ungodliness from godliness? Just
under. That's all!**   254-68

What matters are the choices that bring about
inharmonies, combinations of those elements and destructive manifestations of the One Force. We have a
lot to learn about loving God! It should become the
absorbing concern of every one of us to grow in a
deeper and deeper sense of the meaning of God and of
joyous living in the commandment to love God.

Do we love God? Do we love our neighbor? How
can we grow in our love for God and neighbor? The
A.R.E. has a study group program entitled *A Search
for God*. God is not lost, so we do not have to search for
Him in that sense. We know that He *is love* so "a search
for God" can be paraphrased as "learning how to love."
This is what our program truly is about.

The Edgar Cayce readings say that the most important experience of any entity is first to know the spiritual ideal. Is love our ideal? By an ideal, we mean a
motivational criterion. Love is a motivational criterion,
but is it the measuring rod by which we are willing to

measure our lives? Setting this spiritual ideal for our-selves gives us a standard by which to measure the motivational bases of our decisions. So we must first set the ideal of love.

Second, we must meditate. In meditation using an affirmation we may awaken the authentic spirit of the ideal. Meditation is one of the most pure and direct ways of expressing our love of God. When we love someone deeply, we want especially to be with them, to be near them, to be in their presence. As we grow in our love of God, we grow in our desire to invite and sense His presence daily in the silence. He knocks gently at the door, but He will not be the uninvited guest.

In Book I of *A Search for God*, there are 12 chapters, the last of which is entitled "Love." The others are steps in learning how to love. These steps include Cooperation, Faith, Fellowship, and Patience. Consider the first chapter on Cooperation in dealing with difficult persons. We may say, "I cannot love that person!" but we *can* act toward the person in a more cooperative manner. From the information in this chap-ter, we come to a deeper understanding of the spiritual laws of cooperation. Then, in meditation, we use an affirmation that awakens within us the spirit of cooperation.

Then, third, we must act upon, or apply or live the life of that spirit awakened. This is the triple method of the Search for God program. We specify as a discipline how we intend to act more cooperatively with that person. With the application comes the awareness. We may not act in a loving way because we do not feel love, and we do not want to be hypocritical. However, the reverse may be closer to the way in which the law works. As we perform the loving act, we are in a better position to experience an authentic feeling of love. This principle needs special stress. The deepest and most real pattern of response within us is love, because we are made in the image of love. Between this pattern and the conscious mind are many layers of memories, habits, karmic patterns which interpose when we are confronted with a choice. These may make us feel unloving but if we choose and do the loving act, we enhance the continuing appearance of the true Self patterned after and motivated only by love. Always we should call in His name even if we do not sense His presence, for He is with us always, eager to imbue with His power our choice of His pattern. As we apply, we grow in awareness. And as we become more cooperative, we move on to a new chapter and the unfolding of a new petal in the blossom of love—patience.

From the *A Search for God* text, we learn the laws of patience. In daily meditation working with an affirmation, we awaken the spirit of patience and the energy with which to apply it. Then in specifying a discipline, we act in a more patient way with the person with whom we have to deal. As we begin to understand, energize and apply these attributes, we find that we have indeed come to love this person, who at first seemed so difficult. Thus we have in this program progressive growth steps toward learning how to love.

In study group work, there is always a particularly difficult person. Everyone in the group does not always agree on who that is, but there is always one you have to deal with over a period of weeks or months. As we pray for him every day and meet with him once a week, share experiences with him and discuss spiritual laws with him and try to act in a more loving way a beautiful thing starts to happen—we come to love that "difficult" person. These study groups are workshops and laboratories. We discover that as we begin to apply the principles of love with people in the group, we can apply them to people on the job and in our family. Also, each one of us may be that "difficult" person for someone else. As we set love as an ideal, meditate to awaken the spirit of love and begin to act in a more loving manner, we open ourselves to a powerful and integrative growth process. We learn to understand and feel and act in a more loving way than we ever thought possible.

I know it from personal experience, and from the experience of many others, that this approach to "learning how to love" works.

Finally, let us always be assured that there is an

Enabler in our learning how to love who is, of course, the Spirit of Christ. Would that all might learn that He, the Christ, is the Giver, the Maker, the Creator of the world and all that is therein. We are in Him and He is in us. He is, He was, He ever will be the expression, the concrete expression of love in the earth. He is the standard of love upon which we may rely wholly. The love divine as was manifested in the man Jesus was and ever will be the criterion of judgment upon the consciousness of us all. It is His spirit acting through us, and not we ourselves, that enables us to be assured of growth in our ultimate venture—learning how to love.

From the Infinite into the Finite

The great problem for all religions has been understanding the nature of the relationship between God and man. There are difficulties of terminology as to whether the *Infinite* is to be referred to as the Universe, the Divine, the One, or as God, Om, Yahweh, Allah, or the Void. Nevertheless, the question remains as to the possibility and specific nature of the relationship of the *Infinite* to individual man. This is the query of the psalmist when he asks, "What is man, that Thou art mindful of him?"

One answer to this question, and our central thesis here, is that man may be defined as *a unique portion of the process and a record of the expression of the Infinite into the finite!*

An illustration of this insight into the nature of man is found in a Hindu legend related by W.H. Danforth in *I Dare You:*

> At one time all men on earth were gods, but... men so sinned and abused the Divine that Brahma, the god of all gods, decided that the godhead should be taken away from man and hid some place where he would never again find it and abuse it. "We will bury it deep in the earth," said the other gods. "No," said Brahma, "because man will dig down in the earth and find it." "Then we will sink it in the deepest ocean," they said. "No," said Brahma, "because man will learn to dive and find it

13

there, too." "We will hide it on the highest mountain," they said. "No," said Brahma, "because man will some day climb every mountain on earth and again capture the godhead." "Then we do not know where to hide it where he cannot find it," said the lesser gods. "I will tell you," said Brahma, "hide it down in man himself. He will never think to look there."

And that is what they did. Hidden down in every man is some of the divine. Ever since then he has gone over the earth digging, diving and climbing, looking for that godlike quality which all the time is hidden down within himself.

For me this legend is reminiscent not only of the Biblical stories of the fall of man and the Prodigal Son, but also of the peculiar *way* in which man is "lost" or separated in consciousness from his awareness of the Divine.

Intimations of this theme of the Godhead within are seen in passages from Kahlil Gibran's *The Prophet*.

And a man said, Speak to us of Self-Knowledge.

And he answered, saying:

Your hearts know in silence the secrets of the days and nights.

But your ears thirst for the sound of your heart's knowledge.

You would know in words that which you have always known in thought.

Then said a teacher, Speak to us of Teaching.

And he said:

No man can reveal to you aught but that which already lies half asleep in the dawning of your knowledge.

The teacher who walks in the shadow of the temple, among his followers, gives not of his wisdom but rather of his faith and his lovingness.

If he is indeed wise he does not bid you enter the house of his wisdom, but rather leads you to the threshold of your own mind.

The English poet, Robert Browning, wrote a classically beautiful and instructive passage in which Paracelsus, a seeker of truth, says:

Truth is within ourselves; it takes no rise
From outward things, whate'er you may believe.
There is an inmost centre in us all,
Where truth abides in fulness; and around
Wall upon wall, the gross flesh hems it in,
This perfect, clear perception—which is truth.
A baffling and perverting carnal mesh
Binds it, and makes all error: and, to KNOW,
Rather consists in opening out a way
Whence the imprisoned splendour may escape,
Than in effecting entry for a light
Supposed to be without.

The concepts of "the Godhead within" in the Hindu legend, the "imprisoned splendour" of Browning's poem, the Biblical and contemporary accounts of the spiritual nature of man and his paranormal abilities have been tied together even more clearly by laboratory studies demonstrating the factuality of ESP. There are parallels between the Hindu and the Biblical stories of the fall of man, as well as Browning's "baffling and perverting carnal mesh" and Freud's theory of the neuroses. Freud explained the unconscious as a vast and reprehensible dungeon of the psyche which was also the powerhouse within man, the source of all of his creative and religious impulses.

These concepts all relate to the manner in which the power and knowledge of the Infinite are expressed through finite man, and of the barriers that separate our finite conscious minds from their potential for an awareness of the Infinite. Many who write and talk about the ideas of these different fields of study seem to think of them as being thoroughly disparate. Yet the Hindu legend may help us to imagine that underneath all of these theories and experiences there exists a Oneness—even as in the story of the five blind men of Hindustan who, upon feeling different parts of the same elephant, described it in vastly different terms.

In *There Is a River,* we found the story of a man whose life work was a continuing expression of the potential of the spiritual nature of man. Edgar Cayce manifested, in his thoughts and actions, the harmony of the God without and the Godhead within. Guided by the principle of Oneness, he tried to manifest the spirit of life from the Infinite into the finite. Motivated by the purpose of helplessness to others, he sought to give expression to the flow of energy and information to the Divine without through the Divine within.

For more than forty years, until shortly before his death in 1945, Edgar Cayce conducted a work which has been referred to as "giving readings." The total number of these readings exceeds 14,000. What is an Edgar Cayce "reading"? The definition is, perhaps, determined by the extent to which one is prepared to affirm that the Infinite can express through the finite. For that is what seemed to happen when, in his daily work to help others, Edgar Cayce would lie down, close his eyes and move to a level of consciousness from which information relevant to any question asked was accessible.

The Edgar Cayce readings contribute extraordinary substance and insight to our study of the nature of man. These readings give us a deep and renewed interest in the Bible. Their approach to the Bible is far more profound, more integrated, more viable and applicable, and more universal than anything we may have previously imagined. Especially valuable are the readings' insights and instructions on the inner life. The information on prayer, meditation, dreams and other aids to attunement assure us of the feasibility, practicali-

ty and immeasurable value of our approaching the
Divine within.

Deuteronomy 30, recommended often in Edgar
Cayce's readings, parallels the Hindu legend recounted
above. This chapter in the Bible may really come to life
for us when we discover the insistence of the Edgar
Cayce readings on the chapter's importance and appli-
cability to a great variety of circumstances for people
with widely differing needs.

We are reminded of the Hindu legend by this
passage from Deuteronomy:

> For this commandment which I command
> thee this day, it is not hidden from thee,
> neither is it far off.
>
> It is not in heaven, that thou shouldest
> say, Who shall go up for us to heaven, and
> bring in unto us, that we may hear it, and do
> it?
>
> Neither is it beyond the sea, that thou
> shouldest say, Who shall go over the sea for
> us, and bring it unto us, that we may hear it,
> and do it?
>
> But the word is very nigh unto thee, in
> thy mouth, and in thy heart, that thou mayest
> do it.   (Deuteronomy 30:11-14)

As we trace this theme in the Bible, we find the
prophet Jeremiah saying:

> But this shall be the covenant that I will
> make with the house of Israel; After those
> days, saith the LORD, I will put my law in
> their inward parts, and write it in their hearts,
> and will be their God, and they shall be my
> people.
>
> And they shall teach no more every man
> his neighbor, and every man his brother, saying,
> Know the LORD: for they shall all know me . . .
>   (Jeremiah 31:33-34)

The epistle of Paul to the Hebrews carries the same promise:

> Whereof the Holy Ghost also is a witness to us: for after that he had said before,
> This is the covenant that I will make with them after those days, saith the Lord, I will put my laws into their hearts, and in their minds will I write them . . .
>
> (Hebrews 10:15-16)

We may find this same theme quoted, paraphrased and interpreted in a most challenging and exciting way in Paul's letter to the Romans:

> For Christ is the end of the law for righteousness to everyone that believeth.
> For Moses describeth the righteousness which is of the law, That the man which doeth those things shall live by them.
> But the righteousness which is of faith speaketh on this wise, Say not in thine heart, Who shall ascend into heaven? (that is, to bring Christ down from above:)
> Or, Who shall descend into the deep? (that is, to bring up Christ again from the dead.)
> But what saith it? The word is nigh thee, even in thy heart; that is, the word of faith, which we preach.
>
> (Romans 10:4-8)

For Paul the law of Deuteronomy 30 which is written in our mouths and in our hearts is the Christ which is within us. That law—that is carried in the Ark of the Covenant, the central symbol in the Holy of Holies where the priest was to meet God face to face—that law, the Torah, is the Christ. For Paul, as for Jesus, the body is the temple. There are we to meet Him, within ourselves. And that law, as fulfilled by the Christ and *as* the Christ, is the law of love. It is the pattern of the Divine within each of us waiting to be rediscovered, awakened and lived out in fullness, as He prepared it from the beginning and demonstrated it through His life to be the Way.

As we pursue studies of comparative religions we may continue to find parallel themes in a variety of places. We learn that in Hinduism, the most encompassing name for God is Brahma. Just as in the Old Testament, there is a preference not to use the word because of its limiting effects. Brahma cannot be described but only referred to as "that," or in Sanskrit, *tat*. The Godhead within man is called the Atman, the high self. Yet, Brahma and the Atman are one and the same as taught in the Sanskrit expression, *"tat tvam asi,"* "that, thou art." That Brahma or God or universal principle is the same as the Atman or Christ within, the *true* nature of ourselves.

In his book, *Beyond Theology*, Alan Watts discusses his personal search and why he developed his preference for Hinduism over Christianity. He came to feel that this *tat tvam asi* gave Hinduism an edge over Christianity because of a more inclusive philosophy of God in man. But the Old Testament name, "I Am That I Am," is the same teaching embodying the same principle! When Moses sought from God an authoritative name which he could use to back up the message he was to take to his people, he was told "I Am That I Am." In other words, the source is that "I Am" or Godhead within which is the same essence as the "I AM," or God without.

Sri Aurobindo, an Indian mystic and philosopher, describes the theme in *Essays on the Gita* as the Secret of Secrets. The Great Hindu sacred scriptures of the Bhagavad-Gita tells the story of the student Arjuna taught by Krishna, an incarnation of Vishnu (whose function in the Hindu trinity parallels that of the Christ in Christianity). Aurobindo describes the development of a crucial point in Krishna's teachings:

> All the truth that has developed itself at this length step by step, each bringing forward

a fresh aspect of the integral knowledge and
founding on it some result of spiritual state
and action, has now to take a turn of immense
importance. The Teacher therefore takes care
first to draw attention to the decisive character
of what he is about to say, so that the mind of
Arjuna may be awakened and attentive. For
he is going to open his mind to the knowledge
and sight of the integral Divinity... the Godhead in man and the world, whom nothing in
man and in the world limits or binds, because
all proceeds from him, is a movement in his
infinite being, continues and is supported by
his will, is justified in his divine self-knowledge,
has him always for its origin, substance and
end. Arjuna is to become aware of himself
existing only in God and as acting only by the
power within him, his workings only an in-
strumentality of the divine action, his egotistic
consciousness only a veil and his ignorance a
misrepresentation of the real being within him
which is an immortal spark and portion of the
supreme Godhead... The soul that fails to get
faith in the higher truth and law, must return
into the path of ordinary mortal living subject
to death and error and evil: it cannot grow
into the Godhead which it denies. For this is a
truth which has to be lived—and lived in the
soul's growing light, not argued out in the
mind's darkness. One has to grow into it, one
has to become it—that is the only way to
verify it... But to grow thus into the freedom
of the divine Nature one must accept and
believe in the Godhead secret within our present limited nature.

Tvat tvam asi! ... that, thou art! ... I Am That I
Am! ... You are gods!

Our study of comparative religions may lead us to
an interest in the relevance of Buddhism to our search,
the frequently misunderstood but nevertheless extraor-

dinarily high form of Buddhism developed in Tibet. An example is found in the excellent writing of Lama Govinda. Govinda's *Foundations of Tibetan Mysticism* is probably the most profound and integrative writing extant on Tibetan Buddhism. Here, again, we find exciting insights on our theme.

Although Gautama, the Buddha, knew the Hindu wisdom of the Infinite in the finite, the very theology of it led many to an illusion of separation between "here" and "there." Gautama wanted to experience the oneness. As he did so, in realizing nirvana, he developed one of the greatest approaches in the history of man to his understanding of himself. Yet it is amazing how little we have understood the wisdom of the great teachers of the world. For example, we hear that in Buddhism the goal of man is nirvana. Most of us think of nirvana in terms very much like those used by Sir Edwin Arnold in the closing line of *The Light of Asia:* "The dewdrop slips into the shining sea."

Lama Govinda sees this as a misunderstanding of the goal of Buddhism. He says that it may make beautiful poetry, but it makes very inaccurate philosophy. Govinda continues: "If this beautiful simile is reversed, it would probably come nearer to the Buddhist conception of ultimate realization: it is not the drop that slips into the sea, but the sea that slips into the drop! The universe becomes conscious in the individual (but not vice versa), and it is in this process that completeness is achieved, in regard to which we neither can speak any more of 'individual' nor of 'universe.'"

". . . it is not the drop that slips into the sea but the sea that slips into the drop!" This insight not only recognizes the oneness of the Godhead within and the universe without but it also defines the direction of the flow of energy and consciousness, of life itself. It is not so much that we are to return to God but rather that we are to express the fullness of the nature of God in our present lives.

The Edgar Cayce readings express the same insight in these terms:

Hence, as man applies himself—or uses that of which he becomes conscious in the realm of activity, and gives or places the credit (as would be called) in man's consciousness in the correct sphere or realm he becomes conscious of that union of force with *the infinite with the finite* force.

Hence, in the fruits of that—as is given oft, as the fruits of the spirit—does man become aware of the infinite penetrating, or interpenetrating the activities of all forces of matter, or that which is a manifestation of the realm of *the infinite into the finite*—and the finite becomes conscious of same. [Author's italics]
262-52

The oneness of the Divine without and Divine within, and the direction of the flow from the *Infinite into the finite* . . . this is the central insight regarding the nature of man which may be found in the great sacred literature of the world, whether it be Hindu, Buddhist or Judeo-Christian in origin. Furthermore, when these sacred writings have not only been searched most profoundly, but at the same time lived most fully, the same theme emerges. Contemporary examples of this are found in the mystical philosophies of Sri Aurobindo, the Hindu; Lama Govinda, the Buddhist; and Edgar Cayce, the Judeo-Christian.

We need not be so naive as to be unaware that there are differences in these approaches which to the minds of some are irreconcilable; nevertheless, this ubiquitous secret about the Godhead nature of man seems to be the key to understanding that God is truly *our* Father, and that all men without exception are *brothers* in this divine heritage. However, there is psychological difficulty which may go far deeper than all of the theological problems that may arise from this principle.

If this insight is ubiquitous, why does it remain the Secret of Secrets? Why is this realization the most deeply resisted insight of all mankind? To say that there are resistances to this insight is truly an understatement of our problem. In actuality, when we are confronted

with the *truth* of our Godhead nature, we become
extremely anxious. When such a confrontation is made
by a man like Jesus who awakens a consciousness that
penetrates our amnesic, repressive barriers, we begin
to remember dimly that original divine state from which
we have fallen so far. The pain of self-condemnation can
become so great that it is unbearable; and we project it
outward in murderous rage toward that person who has
awakened in us the memory of that loss. We hurl at
Him the epithet of blasphemy. Psychologically there
can be no doubt that our anger is part of the defense
mechanism of projection mobilized to help us avoid the
pain of a growing awareness, the *real* separation anxiety. We, like the prodigal, "come to ourselves" and
remember that from which we have strayed so far.

Let me dramatize and clarify this point further by
inviting you to move back through 2,000 years to a
first-person encounter with Jesus. Paraphrasing John
10, we find ourselves protesting against the truth, and
the Master trying to help us accept it.

> I and my Father are one.
> Then we took up stones again to stone
> him.
> Jesus answered us, Many good works have
> I shewed you from my Father; for which of
> those works do ye stone me?
> We answered him saying, For a good
> work we stone thee not; but for blasphemy;
> and because that thou, being a man, makest
> thyself God.
> Jesus answered us, Is it not written in
> your law, I said, Ye are gods?
> If he called them gods, unto whom the
> word of God came, and the scripture cannot
> be broken;
> Say ye of him, whom the Father hath
> sanctified, and sent into the world, Thou
> blasphemest; because I said, I am the Son of
> God?   (John 10:30-36)

Jesus was accused of blasphemy for saying, "I and my Father are one," but when He replied by quoting Psalm 82, "Is it not written in your law, I said, Ye are gods?" He made it clear that He was not making special claims about Himself, but rather, was quoting from a highly revered Old Testament source, reminding us of our own divinity. The passage says, ". . . Ye are gods; and all of you are children of the Most High."

This principle, that we are gods, is one of the most important ways of stating the gospel, and it is *good* news indeed. Yet it is not simply news for the intellect. It is for the heart as well. The Word is not lived in the words of our mouths but through the loving spirit of our hearts and the selfless actions of our lives. Thus, this gospel is good news for all men and not the exclusive property of any one hemisphere, civilization, culture or religious organization simply because certain words are used.

The good news is not only that the Word was with God and the Word was God and the Word became flesh and dwelt among us (that is, the Infinite into the finite) but also that He said I call you not servants but friends. (John 15:15) His claim to divinity, a block upon which we seem to enjoy stumbling, was in truth His claim for the divine origin and sonship of all men. Though He said, "If you have seen me you have seen the Father," He also said, "I in the Father and the Father in me and I in you and you in me"—*Oneness*. The question of the divinity of Jesus is answered by the realization that *there is only One and that One is God*. Hear, O Israel, the Lord thy God is *One*.

These passages from various sources illustrate some of the high points in man's search for answers to the questions "What is man?" and "Who am I?" These questions are among the most important we can ask ourselves. It is likely that everyone who examines his own growth will find, in answering these questions, that it has been a growth toward understanding how the Infinite expresses in the finite.

We now restate our primary thesis: Man may be

defined as a *unique portion of the process and a record of the expression of the Infinite into the finite*.

A Biblical Study on the Origin and Destiny of Man

The Master's parable of the prodigal son presents a promising paradigm relating to the origin and destiny of man.

The Parable of the Prodigal Son

And he said, A certain man had two sons:

And the younger of them said to his father, Father, give me the portion of goods that falleth to me. And he divided unto them his living.

And not many days after, the younger son gathered all together, and took his journey into a far country, and there wasted his substance with riotous living.

And when he had spent all, there arose a mighty famine in that land; and he began to be in want.

And he went and joined himself to a citizen of that country; and he sent him into his fields to feed swine.

And he would fain have filled his belly with the husks that the swine did eat; and no man gave unto him.

And when he came to himself, he said, How many hired servants of my father's have bread enough and to spare, and I perish with hunger!

I will arise and go to my father, and will say unto him, Father, I have sinned against heaven, and before thee.

And am no more worthy to be called thy son: make me as one of thy hired servants.

And he arose, and came to his father. But when he was yet a great way off, his father saw him, and had compassion, and ran, and fell on his neck, and kissed him.

And the son said unto him, Father, I have sinned against heaven, and in thy sight, and am no more worthy to be called thy son.

But the father said to his servants, Bring forth the best robe, and put it on him; and put a ring on his hand, and shoes on his feet:

And bring hither the fatted calf, and kill it; and let us eat, and be merry:

For this my son was dead, and is alive again; he was lost, and is found. And they began to be merry.

Now his elder son was in the field: and as he came and drew nigh to the house, he heard music and dancing.

And he called one of the servants, and asked what these things meant.

And he said unto him, Thy brother is come; and thy father hath killed the fatted calf, because he hath received him safe and sound.

And he was angry, and would not go in: therefore came his father out, and entreated him.

And he answering said to his father, Lo, these many years do I serve thee, neither transgressed I at any time thy commandment: and yet thou never gavest me a kid, that I might make merry with my friends:

But as soon as this thy son was come, which hath devoured thy living with harlots, thou hast killed for him the fatted calf.

And he said unto him, Son, thou art ever with me, and all that I have is thine.

It was meet that we should make merry, and be glad: for this thy brother was dead, and is alive again; and was lost, and is found.

(Luke 15:11-32)

The parable of the prodigal son is universally acknowledged to be the ultimate epitome of the pilgrimage of the soul of man. The story may be outlined and diagrammed in five stages:

1. In the beginning he was one with his father, a true heir in his father's house.

2. He asked for his inheritance and left his father by his own choice. He misused his gifts and talents and thereby steadily deteriorated.

3. At a final low point he came to himself and said, "I will arise and go to my father..."

4. When he was yet a great way off, his father saw him and ran to meet him. He confessed his wrongs, but his father embraced him, rejoiced at his return and said, "... this my son was dead, and is alive again."

5. He was given a royal robe and a royal ring to reconfirm his heritage.

His life was fully reestablished in his father's house with much rejoicing even though the attitude of the elder brother saw this as being unfair.

Jesus began the sermon, which includes the parable of the prodigal, with the stories of the lost sheep and the lost coin. All three of these parables feature this sequence: 1) being home; 2) going astray; and 3) returning with rejoicing.

I. The Divine Origin: "A Man Had Two Sons"

The specific sequence of events in the parable of the prodigal has several points in common with other Biblical accounts. The story of Adam and Eve parallels the beginning of the parable of the prodigal son. Created in the image of God and blessed by God, Adam and

Eve were perfect from the outset. However, although they were placed in a paradise called "a garden in Eden, in the east," they, like the prodigal son, strayed from fellowship with their Father by their own choice and became "strangers and exiles on the earth." (II Samuel 15:19) To eat of the tree of knowledge of good and evil meant death. Let us continue to note the way in which death is used to denote separation in consciousness from God. The father of the prodigal spoke of his son as having been dead. The New Testament picks up on the cosmic scope of this story with a joyous outcome; the promise of the full return of the prodigal is given in the assurance: "For as in Adam *all* die, so also in Christ shall *all* be made alive." (I Cor. 15:22)

The story of Job parallels the prodigal son sequence. Job was in fellowship with his Father; God spoke of him as, ". . . a blameless and upright" man. (Job 1:1) Although a lengthy series of difficulties develops, the outcome of Job's life was highly favorable: "And the Lord blessed the latter days of Job more than his beginning . . ." (Job 42:12)

As a paradigm of the origin of man, the prodigal's original state of being faultless and one with the father implies for all of us as souls a previous existence in a state of perfection. An intimation of previous existence is given in the following:

The Lord asks Job, "Where were you when I laid the foundation of the earth? . . . when the morning stars sang together, and all the sons of God shouted for joy?" (Job 38:4-7) The Lord answers this question with another question, according to some translations, such as the King James and the Jerusalem. However, in the Revised Standard and the Jewish Masoretic translations, the Lord answers His own query with an affirmation: "You know, for you were born then, and the number of your days is great!" (Job 38:21)

Another story indicating more directly the divine origin and original perfection of the soul is found in Ezekiel 28, wherein the prophet is sent to the King of Tyre and directed to say to him, "Thus says the Lord God: 'You were the signet of perfection, full of wisdom and perfect in beauty. You were in Eden, the Garden of God; every precious stone was your covering . . . You were blameless in your ways from the day you were created; till iniquity was found in you . . . In the abundance of your trade you were filled with violence, and you sinned; so I cast you as a profane thing from the mountain of God . . . ' " (Ezekiel 28:12-16)

When these three passages are evaluated as instructions regarding generic man, the implications are that:

1. We were created in the image of God.
2. We were perfect and in full fellowship with God in the beginning.
3. We went astray by our own choice.

The Preexistent Christ as the Pattern

The Master's parable of the prodigal has given us a model for considering the origin and destiny of man. Now let us examine the extent to which the experiences of the Master Himself parallel this model.

Let us consider the first chapter of John:

In the beginning was the Word and the Word was with God, and the Word was God.

The same was in the beginning with God.

All things were made by him; and without him was not anything made that was made.

In him was life; and the life was the light of men.

And the light shineth in darkness; and the darkness comprehended it not.

. . . That was the true Light, which lighteth every man that cometh into the world.

He was in the world, and the world was made by him, and the world knew him not.

. . . But as many as received him, to them gave he the power to become the sons of God, even to them that believe on his name:

Which were born, not of blood, nor of the

will of the flesh, nor of the will of man, but of
God.

And the Word was made flesh, and dwelt
among us, (and we beheld his glory, the glory
as of the only begotten of the Father) full of
grace and truth.   (John 1:1-14, KJV)

Several important ideas emerge from this magnificent proclamation.

The Word was with God and the Word was God in
the beginning. This Word, the Christ, was the preexistent
mediator of all creation. This Word, or logos, which was
in the beginning with God and through whom all things
were made is no doubt the personified wisdom of
Proverbs.

The Lord possessed me in the beginning
of his way, before his works of old.

I was set up from everlasting, from the
beginning, or ever the earth was.

When there were no depths, I was brought
forth; when there were no fountains abounding
with water.

Before the mountains were settled, before the hills was I brought forth:

While as yet he had not made the earth,
nor the fields, nor the highest part of the dust
of the world.

When he prepared the heavens, I was
there: when he set a compass upon the face of
the depth:

When he established the clouds above:
when he strengthened the fountains of the
deep:

When he gave to the sea his decree, that
the waters should not pass his commandment:
when he appointed the foundations of the
earth:

Then I was by him, as one brought up

with him: and I was daily his delight, rejoicing
always before him:

Rejoicing in the habitable part of his earth;
and *my delights were with the sons of men*.

Now therefore harken unto me, O ye
children: for blessed are they that keep my
ways.

Hear instruction, and be wise, and refuse
it not.

Blessed is the man that heareth me,
watching daily at my gates, waiting at the
posts of my doors.

For whoso findeth me findeth life, and
shall obtain favour of the Lord.

. . . Come, eat of my bread and drink of
the wine I have mingled.

(Proverbs 8:22-35, 9:5)

The Preexistent Christ who is the Mediator of all
creation is affirmed again in Colossians.

Who is the image of the invisible God,
the firstborn of every creature:

For by him were all things created, that
are in heaven, and that are in earth, visible
and invisible, whether they be thrones, or
dominions, or principalities, or powers: all
things were created by him, and for him:

And he is before all things, and by him all
things consist.

And he is the head of the body, the
church: who is the beginning, the firstborn
from the dead; that in all things he might have
preeminence.   (Colossians 1:15-18)

Why is He said to have been "the firstborn from
the dead"? Why is the term "dead" applied to Him, as
it was to the prodigal and to Adam and Eve? Why is it
said of Him, "Although he was a Son, he learned
obedience through what he suffered . . ."? (Hebrews 5:8)
Wherein was His need for learning obedience?

> But now is Christ risen from the dead,
> and become the firstfruits of *them that slept*.
>
> For since by man came death, by man
> came also the resurrection of the dead.
>
> For as in Adam all die, even so in Christ
> shall all be made alive. (I Corinthians 15:20-22)

The expression, "firstfruits of them that slept," seems to refer to the same quality as, "the firstborn of the dead..."

Notice also that it is said of Him, "For it was fitting that he, for whom and by whom all things exist, in bringing many sons to glory, should make the pioneer of their salvation perfect through suffering. For he who sanctifies and those who are sanctified *have all one origin*. That is why he is not ashamed to call them brethren..." (Hebrews 2:10-11, RSV)

Wherein was the need of making Him perfect through suffering? Our brotherhood is implied and then affirmed in this passage—we are all of one *origin*.

Peter spoke of Him as one, "Who verily was foreordained before the foundation of the world..." (I Peter 1:20) like Melchisedek, who "has neither beginning of days nor end of life..." (Hebrews 7:3) He was prophesied to be one "... whose goings forth have been from of old, from everlasting." (Micah 5:2) These "goings forth" may be that referred to when He says, "Your father Abraham rejoiced that he was to see my day; and he saw it and was glad... Truly, truly, I say to you, before Abraham was, I am." (John 8:56-58)

We know that Abraham, who was held in extraordinarily high esteem by his descendants, paid tithes to Melchisedek "... king of Salem... priest of God most High," who "... brought out bread and wine," as did the Master. (Genesis 14:18-20) Was this the occasion when "Abraham rejoiced to see his day"? Certainly, we are told of His pre-Jesus work in the earth in certain passages of scripture. Moses, it is said, "... considered abuse suffered for the Christ greater wealth than the treasures of Egypt..." (Hebrews 11:26) Those with Moses "... drank from the supernatural Rock which followed them, and the Rock was Christ." (I Corinthians 10:4)

The passages given above illustrate the preexistent or pre-Jesus work of the Christ both as the mediator of creation and as working in the ongoing pilgrimage of man. They show Him incarnate, suffering, learning obedience and being the firstborn of the dead. And they show Him to be our brother, of "one origin." Therefore the paradigm, as we see it in the stories of Adam, of the prodigal and of Job is the pattern of the Master as well as of ourselves. Several questions are raised here; let us consider primarily the incarnation of the Divine.

The Incarnation of the Divine

The scandal of the New Testament is the teaching of the incarnation of God, ". . . and the Word ("which was with God and was God," John 1:1) became flesh and dwelt among us..." (John 1:14) This question of the incarnation is a crucial one, not only in understanding Jesus but even more so in understanding ourselves as children of God, brothers of Jesus. We were outraged when He said, "I and the Father are one." (John 10:30) But did He not reply, "Is it not written in your law, 'I said, you are gods'? If He called them gods to whom the word of God came (and scripture cannot be broken), do you say of him whom the father consecrated, and sent into the world, 'you are blaspheming,' because I said, 'I am the Son of God'?" (John 10:34-36)

The anxiety-arousing issue was ". . . blasphemy; because you, being a man, made yourself God." His epochal reply was a quotation from the 82nd Psalm in which God is quoted as having said, "You are gods, sons of the Most High, all of you..." To the much-challenged claim of the divinity of Jesus, His own reply was a claim for the divine nature of us all... "You are gods."

II. The Fall: "He Wasted His Substance"

Jesus' reaffirmation of the divine nature of man clearly places the parable of the prodigal in a position for even more serious consideration. The incarnation of the divine then refers not only to Jesus but also to all of us as gods, brethren of him, and all of one origin. In the parable of the prodigal, the son went astray of his own choice. If we accept Jesus' teaching that we are gods and that we are His brothers, if we accept His parable as a model for the pilgrimage of the soul, then we can look more seriously at the nature of the fall. In at least four instances in scripture where there is a statement about our divine origin—that we are gods—there is also a statement immediately afterwards that our biggest problem relates to our own response to the gift of divine heritage.

1. Adam and Eve partook of the tree of the knowledge of good and evil because the serpent said, "... ye shall be as gods..." (Genesis 3:5, KJV) or "... you will be like God..." (RSV) Apparently the Lord confirmed the problem of the promise of the serpent because after they had partaken of it, God said, "'Behold, the man has become like one of us knowing good and evil; and now, lest he put forth his hand and take also of the tree of life, and eat, and live forever': Therefore the Lord God sent him forth from the garden..." (Genesis 3:22-23)

2. In the 82nd Psalm, a great gathering is portrayed: "God standeth in the congregation of the mighty; he judgeth among the gods." He says, because "... ye judge unjustly... all the foundations of the earth are out of course. I have said, Ye are gods; and all of you are children of the most high. But ye shall die like men, and fall like one of the princes." (Psalm 82:1, 2, 5-7)

3. In Isaiah, Lucifer is addressed by the Lord in a similar accusation:

> How art thou fallen from heaven, O Lucifer, son of the morning! how art thou cut down to the ground, which didst weaken the nations!
>
> For thou hast said in thine heart, *I will* ascend into heaven, *I will* exalt my throne above the stars of God: *I will* sit also upon the mount of the congregation, in the sides of the north:

I will ascend above the heights of the clouds; *I will* be like the most High.

Yet thou shalt be brought down to hell, to the sides of the pit.   (Isaiah 14:12-14, KJV)

4. In the account in Ezekiel, the Lord admonishes the King of Tyre by saying, "Because thine heart is lifted up and thou hast said, "I am a God, . . . thou shalt die." (Ezekiel 28:2, 10) When Eve ". . . took of the fruit thereof, and did eat, and gave also unto her husband with her; and he did eat" (Genesis 3:6), when those of the congregation of the mighty ". . . judge unjustly. . ." (Psalm 82:2), when Lucifer said, ". . . I will. . ." (Isaiah 14:13), when the King of Tyre said, ". . . I am a God . . ." (Ezekiel 28:2), the spirit of rebellion and sin thus entered.

To be sure, many interpreters of these passages about Adam, Lucifer and the King of Tyre utilize the external projection mechanism and refer them to only one being. However, when we approach these texts as depicting aspects of *generic* man, we find them to be highly instructive regarding not only the nature of the fall but also our own present core of evil. We are Adam, we are the congregation of the mighty, we are the fallen Lucifer, and we are the King of Tyre. Remember, Hebrews 2:11 says, "For he who sanctifies and those who are sanctified have all one origin . . ." and the Master Himself said, "Ye are gods." (John 10:34)

In these three accounts, Genesis 3, Isaiah 14 and Psalm 82, the following view of the nature and problem of man is depicted.

We are children of God, made in His image, we were with Him when the morning stars sang together, and all the sons of God shouted for joy, we were perfect in our ways until fault was found in us because we wanted to be gods apart from God, apart from the Whole and the One. In this pride, this hubris, this spirit of rebellion, we removed ourselves from perfect awareness of the Oneness. The spirit of the loving, creating Father said, "Let us create . . ." Ours became the spirit of Lucifer who said, "I will." As prodigals, we

took our divine heritage, free will, and went astray with
it.

Herein is a *paradox: we are* gods, yet we have
fallen from that state because we wanted to be God.
The resolution of this paradox lies in the spirit of
obedience as it was said of the Master, ". . . yet learned
he obedience." (Hebrews 5:8)

> Let this mind be in you, which was also
> in Christ Jesus:
> Who, being in the form of God, thought
> it not robbery to be equal with God:
> But made himself of no reputation, and
> took upon him the form of a servant, and was
> made in the likeness of men:
> And being found in fashion as a man, he
> humbled himself, and became obedient unto
> death, even the death of the cross.
>
> (Philippians 2:5-8)

When the prodigal said, "I will arise," remember-
ing he was a child of his father, that is, "in the form of
God," he also said, "make me a servant," symbolizing
the need to humble himself and become obedient.

The Seeking Shepherd

Considering that high cosmic state from which we
fell in separating ourselves from Him, the Tree of Life,
we may truly say of our present state, we are dead. But
a voice comes from the Father,

> Repent, and turn yourselves from all your
> transgressions; so iniquity shall not be your
> ruin.
> Cast away from you all your transgres-
> sions, whereby ye have transgressed; and make
> you a new heart and a new spirit: for why will
> ye die, O house of Israel?
> For I have no pleasure in the death of

him that dieth, saith the Lord God: wherefore
turn yourselves, and live ye. (Ezekiel 18:30-32)

And as He said in His story of the lost sheep: "What
man of you, having an hundred sheep, if he lose one of
them, doth not leave the ninety and nine in the wilderness, and go after that which is lost, until he find it?"
(Luke 15:4)

III. The Turning About: "He Came to Himself"

Even though He will ". . . go after that which is
lost, until He find it" (Luke 15:4), the crucial turning
point for us as individual prodigals is illustrated in the
story . . . "he came to himself," and he said, "I will arise
and go to my father." (Luke 15:17-18) Few have been
clear about why a man like John the Baptist was God's
choice of a harbinger for a man like Jesus. But the
spiritual instructions are clear. A strong repentance,
casting out the lower self and bringing forth fruits meet
for repentance is the requisite preparation for the way
of the Lord. We must turn about, come to ourselves
and say, "I will arise and go to my Father."

Jesus set the pattern for this turning point of
repentance and resurrection from the dead by requesting
John to baptize Him. In doing this, He showed that all
without exception are dead and are in need of repentance and rebirth.

Immediately following this, the Spirit of God
descended upon Him like a dove. Many believers
might think of an experience such as the baptism of the
Holy Spirit and the approving voice of God as being the
ultimate crowning experience. For Jesus, who is the
pattern for us all, it was the beginning. Immediately
afterward there was the temptation, then the great
ministry to others accompanied by rejection and humil-
iation, and finally the complete experiencing of the
death and resurrection, symbolized by John's baptism
of Jesus.

IV. The Return: "My Son Is Alive Again"

Finally, having overcome the world and death, Jesus ". . . was received up into heaven, and sat on the right hand of God." (Mark 16:19) But He who sat on the right hand of God also called us brothers (Hebrews 2:11) saying, "To him that overcometh will I grant to sit with me in my throne, even as I also overcame, and am set down with my Father in his throne." (Revelation 3:21)

In John 3:13, Jesus said, "And no man hath ascended up to heaven, but he that came down from heaven, even the Son of man which is in heaven." And in Ephesians 4:9-10 we are told, "Now that he ascended, what is it but that he also descended first into the lower parts of the earth? He that descended is the same also that ascended up far above all heavens . . ." Are not these passages calculated to invite us to consider that to go to a spiritual dimension, one must originally be a spiritual being from a spiritual dimension? Thus, does not our hope and desire for going to heaven reside in our having come from that spiritual home?

What then is our destiny? We are assured that "The Lord is not slack concerning his promise." (II Peter 3:9) "In hope of eternal life, which God, that cannot lie, promised before the world began." (Titus 1:2) ". . . but is long-suffering to us-ward, not willing that any should perish . . ." (II Peter 3:9) If God does not will that any should perish, will any perish? "If God be for us, who can be against us? . . . Who shall lay anything to the charge of God's elect? It is God that justifieth. Who is he that condemneth? . . . Who shall separate us from the love of Christ?" (Romans 8:31, 33, 34, 45)

The Elect

Who are God's elect? Has God elected, or chosen, or even predestined one group of people to the exclusion of others? We are told that God is no respecter of persons. What is meant by the expression, "the elect"?

Here is a "... mystery, which was kept secret since the world began, But now is made manifest, and by the scriptures of the prophets, according to the commandment of the everlasting God, made known to all nations for the obedience of faith." (Romans 16:25-26)

Who are the elect? In Deuteronomy 7:6, we are told of a "... holy people unto the Lord thy God: the Lord hath chosen thee to be a special people unto himself..." The psalmist said, "Blessed is the nation whose God is the Lord; and the people whom he hath chosen for his own inheritance." (Psalm 33:12) "And he brought forth his people with joy, and his chosen with gladness." (Psalm 105:43) "... O visit me with thy salvation; that I may see the good of thy chosen, that I may rejoice in the gladness of thy nation, that I may glory with thine inheritance." (Psalm 106:4-5) To these pleas for salvation, the Lord responds to His chosen as is illustrated in these passages from Isaiah 43 and 44:

Remember ye not the former things, neither consider the things of old.

Behold, I will do a new thing; now it shall spring forth: shall ye not know it? I will even make a way in the wilderness, and rivers in the desert.

The beast of the field shall honour me, the dragons and the owls: because I give waters in the wilderness, and rivers in the desert, to give drink to my people, my chosen.

This people have I formed for myself; they shall shew forth my praise. I even I, am he that blotteth out thy transgressions for mine own sake, and will not remember thy sins...

Thy first father hath sinned, and thy teachers have transgressed against me.

Yet now hear, O Jacob my servant; and Israel, whom I have chosen:

Thus saith the Lord that made thee, and formed thee from the womb, which will help thee; Fear not, O Jacob, my servant; and thou, Jesurun, whom I have chosen.

For I will pour waters upon him that is
thirsty, and floods upon the dry ground: I will
pour my spirit upon thy seed, and my blessing
upon thine offspring.

(Isaiah 43:18-21, 27, 44:1-3)

In Isaiah 45:4, the elect are referred to as *Israel*
but in the New Testament, we are to receive a new
interpretation of the meaning of Israel and thus of the
meaning of God's elect and chosen people. First it must
be clearly understood, as indicated in Isaiah 43, that
election is by grace and not by works. This principle
correlates with the parables in the way in which the
shepherd persists in seeking the lost sheep and in the
way the rejoicing father runs out to meet the returning
prodigal. The Lord said, "... thou hast wearied me
with thine iniquities. I even I, am he that blotteth out
thy transgressions for mine own sake." (Isaiah 43:24-25)
"... that the purpose of God according to election
might stand, not of works, but of him that calleth ... So
then it is not of him that willeth, nor of him that
runneth, but of God that sheweth mercy." (Romans
9:11, 16)

In Romans 11:5-7, we are told of "... the election
of grace. And if by grace then is it no more of works:
otherwise grace is no more grace. But if it be of works,
then it is no more grace: otherwise work is no more
work. What then? Israel hath not obtained that which
he seeketh for; but the election hath obtained it ..."
Israel, the elect and chosen of God! Who are they?

V. *Restoration of the Heritage: "Put a Ring on His Hand"*

We have previously referred to "... the mystery,
which was kept secret since the world began ..." (Romans 16:25) This mystery is now discussed more fully in
Ephesians, third chapter:

If ye have heard of the dispensation of the
grace of God which is given me to you-ward:

How that by revelation he made known unto me the mystery; (as I wrote afore in few words,

Whereby, when ye read, ye may understand my knowledge in the mystery of Christ)

Which in other ages was not made known unto the sons of men, as it is now revealed unto his holy apostles and prophets by the Spirit;

That the Gentiles should be fellowheirs, and of the same body, and partakers of his promise in Christ by the gospel:

Whereof I was made a minister, according to the gift of the grace of God given unto me by the effectual working of his power.

Unto me, whom am less than the least of all saints, is this grace given, that I should preach among the Gentiles the unsearchable riches of Christ;

And to make *all men* see what is the fellowship of the mystery, which from the beginning of the world hath been hid in God, who created all things by Jesus Christ:

To the intent that now unto the principalities and powers in heavenly places might be known by the church the manifold wisdom of God.

According to the eternal purpose which he purposed in Christ Jesus our Lord.

(Ephesians 3:2-11)

The mystery of Christ, ". . . which in other ages was not made known to the sons of men," was that *all*, Israel and Gentiles alike, ". . . should be fellowheirs and of the same body and partakers of his promise in Christ." (Ephesians 3:4, 5, 6) "And to make all men see what is the fellowship of the mystery which from the beginning of the world hath been hid in God, who created all things by Jesus Christ . . . of whom the whole family in heaven and earth is named." (Ephesians 3:9, 15)

The great promise is Oneness—fellowship, fellow-heirs, brotherhood. "There is one body, and one Spirit... One Lord, one faith, one baptism, One God and Father of *all*, who is above *all*, and through *all* and in you *all*... Till we *all* come in the unity of the faith, and of the knowledge of the Son of God, unto a perfect man, unto the measure of the stature of the fullness of Christ." (Ephesians 4:4-6, 13) To "God's elect" is the "... hope of eternal life, which God, that cannot lie, promised before the world began." (Titus 1:1, 2)

God created man, the souls of all men, in His image. He "... created all things by Jesus Christ... Of whom the whole family in heaven and earth is named." (Ephesians 3:9, 15) Therefore, all are of one origin, all are fellowheirs, all are brothers; and, by the love and grace of God, *all* are the elect!

Now having considered that "... the *fellowship* of the mystery, which from the beginning of the world hath been hid in God..." (Ephesians 3:9) is the *election by grace to sonship of all that He created in His image,* we may consider those promises given regarding the destiny of man:

Blessed be the God and Father of our Lord Jesus Christ, who hath blessed us with all spiritual blessings in heavenly places in Christ:

According as he hath chosen us in him before the foundation of the world, that we should be holy and without blame before him in love:

Having predestinated us unto the adoption of children by Jesus Christ to himself, according to the good pleasure of his will,

To the praise of the glory of his grace, wherein he hath made us accepted in the beloved.

In whom we have redemption through his blood, the forgiveness of sins, according to the riches of his grace;

Wherein he hath abounded toward us all in wisdom and prudence;

Having made known unto us the mystery of his will, according to his good pleasure which he hath purposed in himself:

That in the dispensation of the fulness of times he might gather together in one all things in Christ, both which are in heaven, and which are on earth; even in him:

In whom also we have obtained an inheritance, being predestinated according to the purpose of him who worketh all things after the counsel of his own will. (Ephesians 1:3-11)

And we know that all things work together for good to them that love God, to them who are the called according to his purpose.

For whom he did foreknow, he also did predestinate to be conformed to the image of his Son, that he might be the firstborn among many brethren.

Moreover whom he did predestinate, them he also called: and whom he called, them he also justified: and whom he justified, them he also glorified.

What shall we then say to these things? If God be for us, who can be against us?

He that spared not his own Son, but delivered him up for us all, how shall he not with him also freely give us all things?

Who shall lay anything to the charge of God's elect? It is God that justifieth.

(Romans 8:28-33)

Now we may affirm with new confidence, ". . . that he which hath begun a good work in you will perform it until the day of Jesus Christ." (Philippians 1:6)

We were created in His image! It is our destiny to be conformed to that image! If we believe in an all-loving and all-powerful God, no other outcome would make any sense. And there is nothing that can prevent this ultimate transformation for:

> Who shall separate us from the love of Christ? shall tribulation, or distress, or persecution, or famine, or nakedness, or peril, or sword?
> As it is written, For thy sake we are killed all the day long; we are accounted as sheep for the slaughter.
> Nay, in all things we are more than conquerors through him that loved us.
> For I am persuaded, that neither death, nor life, nor angels, nor principalities, nor powers, nor things present, nor things to come,
> Nor height, nor depth, nor any other creature, shall be able to separate us from the love of God, which is in Christ Jesus our Lord. (Romans 8:35-39)

Now let us rejoice in the promise of the parable of the prodigal as it traces in cosmic perspective, the pilgrimage of the Origin and Destiny of all of us and of our Brother the Christ. While we are yet a great way off, our Father sees us, has compassion, and runs out to meet us, eager to restore to us our divine heritage.

Reincarnation,
Psychology
and Christianity

For more than 20 years Edgar Cayce conducted psychic work for medical diagnosis, not mentioning reincarnation until 1911. Then in 1923, two or three questions were asked that stimulated a response in the readings about this vital concept.

Although the word "reincarnation" is so much associated with the Cayce information, we are not trying to teach it as a doctrine. The readings discourage us from trying to convince anyone of it because the approach to reincarnation found in this information is practical and applicable, not theoretical. In one reading, the Cayce source told a person "simply to know you have lived and died and were buried under the cherry tree in grandmother's garden doesn't make you one whit a better person. But, if you can learn that you hurt someone and have suffered and have a chance to make that right, then that's worthwhile." So we are told, if it makes you a better person, work with it as a concept. If not, leave it alone. Thus we approach reincarnation not so much as a theory to be argued out philosophically or theologically but rather as a practical and useful concept.

Both science, especially psychology, and religion, especially Christianity, may find special utility for this concept. And, in inviting scientists and religionists to see if the concept throws some light on their respective fields, I want to discuss some considerations relative to these fields of thought.

It is tempting when the word "reincarnation" is considered, to use the word "belief" with it, such as, "Do you believe in reincarnation?" This question reminds me of another one a few hundred years old, "Do you believe the earth is round?" There were as many arguments about this subject. The great Martin Luther is reported to have said, "Of course the earth is flat. Any fool can see that." An extraordinary theological debate evolved from the question with scriptural reference to the four corners of the earth versus Biblical hints that the earth is spherical. This question, like the reincarnation question, is not one of belief but one of fact. Either life works that way or it doesn't.

Some people think of reincarnation as being something you can opt to believe in or not, as if it makes little difference and there is no way of obtaining facts anyway. In the philosophy of science, these are sometimes called pseudo-problems. When I studied the philosophy of science in 1960, one of the illustrations used of a pseudo-problem was "what does the back side of the moon look like?" They said this was not really a scientific problem because there was no way of observing it. The question now is not speculative and theoretical at all since it can be observed with the new technology. The same may be said of reincarnation. There do exist methodologies for studying this area of human experience and there are facts to be considered. However, most people think of their own personal experience as inclusive of all that may be known about such subjects.

Our experience is that the earth is flat, it is stable, it does not rotate, it does not go anywhere. The sun comes up in the east and it goes down in the west. Hundreds and thousands of years of man's experience seem to probe it is just the way we experience it. The earth is flat. Many people confuse science with experience and common sense. One may say, "I am a scientist. I am hard-nosed about things. I have got to see it to believe it."

You may remember sitting on a beach seeing sails growing up out of the water; then suddenly, a few minutes later, there was the ship. How many times in the past two or three thousand years must men have sat and watched a ship come in, first seeing the mast and then the rest of the ship. Why had it not occurred to man, "Of course, the earth is round!" Sigmund Freud, in writing about the Copernician revolution, says that we can't do justice to thinking about the extraordinary quality of the minds of those men who, after centuries of tradition, questioned the shape of the earth. Imagine a person thinking such a thought in those times and then going about gathering data.

Scientific discoveries are sometimes quite contrary to our perceptions and personal experiences. This comparison of attitudes about reincarnation and the shape of the world interests me because it seems we have a "flat earth" theory about the nature of man today. The meaningfulness of human life supposedly enters at birth and goes out at death. We must be careful even talking about anything before birth or after death because we may drop off the ends.

It may never occur to us, even if we are deeply Christ-oriented and talk about life after death and the resurrection of the body, that if the soul can exist beyond the death of the body, perhaps it had its origin before the body. Do we, as souls who are to live through eternity, just pop into being at the moment of conception? There is far stronger evidence to the contrary than just watching a ship appear on the horizon. In other words, there are many facts which, if we would look at them as such, do indicate a previous existence of the soul.

When we talk about facts, or scientific facts, some will say, "Well, it has not been proven" when what they mean is they have never seen the proof. We have a feeling that unless we ourselves have heard of something, it cannot have been very important. "Edgar Cayce—he couldn't be very important. I've never heard of him before." Later you may discover that millions of people have in fact been helped significantly by this loving man. So, just because we have not heard of something, or have not been willing to work with it, or have made up our minds too quickly, does not necessarily indicate that there are no real facts about its existence or importance.

Very much related to the concept of reincarnation is ESP and telepathy. Some fascinating research was done several years ago on ESP and telepathy in a survey of American psychologists. About 90% at the time (the figure would be lower now) said, "There is nothing to support the idea of ESP or telepathy." Approximately 90% of these same psychologists acknowledged in the questionnaire that they had never read research reports or technical journals in the field of parapsychology. In other words, this group of psychologists, who represent themselves as being scientists, were willing to take a strong position on a question while at the same time acknowledging that they had not even looked at the scientific literature in the field. Surely the scientific attitude should be an open-minded one or at least it should be quite modest about any field studied.

Let us consider a more scientific approach to reincarnation. Dr. Ian Stevenson, a psychiatrist at the University of Virginia, is a widely accepted and highly objective researcher who did some early work with hypnosis. Once, in working with a patient, he began to see intimations of previous life experiences. He decided to investigate the information scientifically and objectively. He felt that hypnosis was not a good approach because of certain problems with the technique. He decided on a case history approach in which facts could be corroborated by objective witnesses.

Prior to publishing his first article on ESP, Dr. Stevenson published an article entitled, "Scientists with Half-Closed Minds." He reviewed the history of science, showing that with great regularity, major breakthroughs in the sciences were resisted by the whole scientific community. When Pasteur said a cow can be killed by a microbe, a little thing you cannot even see, the whole scientific community laughed at him. Pasteur's experience was a typical indicator that scientists are not known to be open-minded. But the *real* scientist, the one who makes the breakthrough, has some *curiosity* and can see beyond the bounds of a flat earth.

With another example from the history of science, Dr. Stevenson makes a point which is relevant to the reincarnation question. He states that the whole scientific community denied for many years the factuality of meteorites even though these men were holding meteorites in their hands, rocks that had made holes in the roofs of houses. The interesting point to note is that those scientists denied the facts not because of the absence of scientific data but because of the feared theological implications. It is a matter of fact that there was a debate then in the natural sciences about whether God intervened in the ongoing natural laws in the earth plane. The argument was that, "Yes, maybe God created this world and He set it in motion, but there are natural laws now that have taken over and God doesn't interfere." They feared that the theory of meteorites would imply that God was altering natural law because some force outside the earth was being introduced. Notice this: scientists made an issue of not accepting the objective data on meteorites because of some feared theological implications. This surely seems naive to us at the present time; however, we have the same situation with reincarnation. One of the problems about objective research on reincarnation is, to be sure, the misgivings some hold about theological implications of the theory.

In his book, *Twenty Cases Suggestive of Reincarnation*, Dr. Stevenson reports on instances of reincarnation recall. Although the book cites only 20 cases, he has investigated more than a thousand objective cases all over the globe—Indians, Eskimos, Iranians, Americans, etc. These cases appear not only in the countries where reincarnation is taught but also in many places where this concept is not known.

When a child begins to talk about previous life memories, there is with great regularity considerable resistance on the part of the family, or the alleged former family, to get involved in establishing the facts. If the child begins to recall a previous life, some very difficult problems may surface. To whom does the child belong if he wants to live with his former family? Even more difficult are cases in which some criminal act may be involved.

The following is an illustration of one of Dr. Stevenson's cases: Ravi Shankar's recall caused great difficulties to both families. This is his story. A little boy named Moona was found dead with his throat cut. Initially, there was a confession from one of the two men involved, a barber and a washerman. The barber, using a razor, had slit the boy's throat in the expectation that it would put him in a better position for an upcoming inheritance. Later, when the trial came up, he claimed that the confession had been made under duress. There was no other evidence of his guilt, no witnesses, so he was found innocent. Just six months after the death of Moona, Ravi Shankar was born some distance away. At about the age of four, he began specifying his former name and the conditions under which he was killed. He gave the name of his previous father and the names of the two alleged murderers, saying they were the washerman and the barber. He said he had been eating guavas before he was murdered, which was the case. He had been enticed to play a game with the men and later it was discovered that either the washerman or the barber had, in fact, been known to play this game with Moona. Ravi Shankar claimed he was killed in an orchard, and this is where Moona's body was found. He said the murderers had buried him in the sand, and this was partially true. He said he had had a bag for his books, an inkpot, a toy pistol, a wooden elephant, a toy doll of the Lord Krishna, a ball attached to an elastic string, a watch and a ring given to him by his father which was in his father's desk. Every one of these details was confirmed and acknowledged. The chances of such correspondences being accidental are astronomical.

So, what about proof? In the history of science, one almost never finds what might be called the critical experiment which in and of itself proves a theory. It is always longed for by a scientific researcher but he will not find it. No single experiment can be found which, if taken alone, would prove the earth is round. Even a photograph taken from outer space does not necessarily constitute "proof." Scientists speak in terms of "evidence in support of" rather than "proof." Scientific progress is made by putting facts together, looking at their implications, and then conducting further experiments. We, therefore, need not say that reincarnation has been proved. However, there are many solid facts in support of this concept.

What are some of the implications of these findings for science? There are several reasons why the science of psychology needs the concept of reincarnation. One of these is the need to think through concepts of guilt and responsibility. Presently, the materialistic and scientific thinking about man is based on a concept that all behavior is determined, almost fixed, by two factors—heredity and environment. For many years, it has been clear that the scientific (physicalistic) world view rules out the concept of free will. As behavioral scientists are appearing more and more in the courts as expert witnesses, the concept that all behavior is determined has led to a considerable eroding of individual responsibility.

There are now numerous criminal cases in which the behavioral scientists have maintained there were so many factors in the background of an individual that these determinants would lead, as a natural consequence, to committing crimes of violence. At a recent American Psychiatric Association Convention, the relationship between criminology and psychiatry was discussed. At this point, they said the problem of criminal responsibility looms large, for, if the deterministic view of mental illness and criminality is to be granted, then criminal responsibility becomes meaningless. It appears that determinism is an arch enemy of the legal system whose major assumption regarding the nature of man involves free will or freedom of choice. If determinism is followed to its logical conclusion, all behaviors are ultimately determined, in part at least, by unconscious processes. Then the question is, of course, whether anybody is guilty of anything, from the legal point of view. Criminal responsibility thus disappears.

Now this is the direction, a strong direction, in the movement of the confrontation between the legal system and the behavioral scientists of our time. I would not speculate about what would happen in our country if the legal and judicial system collapsed but if the question came to the Supreme Court today the present scientific view would require the conclusion that no one could be held responsible for his behavior. Free will? There is hardly a major psychologist of our time who uses the concept of will at all because it has not been a part of scientific world view and movement. The argument for all of your behavior being determined by heredity and environment is very strong. Consider the dire nature of the circumstances in which most of the people of this world are born and raised. We truly cannot talk meaningfully about choices or responsibility without introducing previous existence as the basis for the entity finding himself in such limiting and determining circumstances.

Another problem with which I have been more directly concerned, as a psychotherapist, is the implication of our views on responsibility in counseling with people. If heredity and environment are the determinants of my behavior, then an almost inescapably subjective—and paranoid—response says, "I am in this trouble because *they* didn't give me the right heredity, and *they* didn't give me the right training experiences." Beginning with psychoanalysis and Freud in 1900 and working up to the present day, it is almost unavoidable that anyone who goes to a psychotherapist will receive some of this orientation.

It has also been my experience in psychotherapy that the person who comes to me with the feeling that he *has* been responsible for himself, also feels that he is responsible for change. However, the more imbedded the conviction is that I'm in trouble because "they" made mistakes, the more there is the notion that *they* are the ones who must change. The one who comes and says, "I am having all this trouble because my husband is such a beast," is not as likely to make progress in psychotherapy as the one who says, "I've got to do something about my life."

The Hebrews were dealing with this question as far back as the times of Ezekiel, several hundred years before Jesus: "What mean ye, that ye use this proverb . . . saying 'The fathers have eaten sour grapes and the children's teeth are set on edge? As I live,' saith the Lord God, 'ye shall not have occasion any more to use this proverb in Israel . . . the soul that sinneth, it shall die.' " (Ezekiel 18:2-4) In other words, we are not to say we are in trouble because of our father's difficulties. In this same book, God says to Ezekiel, ". . . Say unto the prince of Tyrus, . . . Thou hast been in Eden the Garden of God . . . Thou wast perfect in thy ways from the day that thou wast created, till iniquity was found in thee." (Ezekiel 28:2, 13, 15) The ancient Hebrews were working not only with the concept of reincarnation but also with some of the behavioral and attitudinal implications of blaming one's difficulties on someone else.

Psychology and psychotherapy are in need of a concept that will enable us to recognize individual responsibility. We cannot find that concept in the context of the present-day materialistic, physicalistic, scientific world view. Within the confines of this scientific viewpoint, the behavioral scientist is right. We cannot be held responsible for our behavior. Externally, this view moves us toward undermining the whole judicial system and internally it works toward a very pathological notion, no matter how small it may be within us, that we are in trouble because of factors for which we are not responsible.

Science, especially psychology, is in need of the reincarnation concept. It is important to reintroduce the concept of will, choice and individual responsibility as they relate to mental hygiene within the individual and to the stability of the moral and legal system in our society.

Now let us consider the religious question. A

young man who had just graduated from a theological seminary wrote an article about reincarnation and the Bible. Even though he raised the question: "Is reincarnation in the Bible?" he really did not address the issue at all. When I met him, I asked him about the article. He said, "Well, you cannot say what's in the Bible just by reading it. We must study patristics, to discern what the early Church fathers said about reincarnation." When I went back to his article to examine it more carefully, I discovered he had reported on only the Church fathers whose views were in accord with contemporary thinking. If we make an unbiased study of the views of the Church fathers of the first and second century following Jesus, we find a great deal of information about reincarnation.

What does the Bible really say? Present-day theologians do not agree. Christian theologians, colleagues within the same church, do not even agree on whether there is the survival of some portion of us following bodily death. The Church and some theologians are sometimes more comfortable with someone who says, "There is no survival," than they are with someone who talks about reincarnation. Some maintain that the ancient Hebrews did not believe in survival.

They speak of the world view of the ancient Hebrews as being the essential basis of our faith. Even if we could reconstruct such a world view, which we cannot, we still would not find a unified view. People today, people a hundred years ago, people 2,000 years ago, even at the top of the main line of thought, do not always agree on certain issues. We cannot say there was a unified world view regarding survival of the soul. Surely the leaders of the temple or synagogue were not always in agreement with the Old Testament prophets. There was always controversy just as there was in the New Testament wherein the Pharisees, the Sadducees and others in positions of authority rejected the teachings of Jesus.

We are addressing the question of orthodoxy, whether it constitutes any kind of satisfactory criterion and whether there has ever been any orthodoxy at all.

When we talk with people, or read books, we do not
tend to find consistency of belief. In the Catholic
Church, there are as many variations of orders as there
are denominations in Protestantism. Some of these are
almost militantly in contradiction with each other. They
are far from being in agreement theologically. A search
for a kind of golden age of belief to use as a criterion for
what may properly be called Christian will be fruitless.

Josephus Flavius was a Jewish historian living in
the times of Jesus, whose book, *Antiquities of the Jews*,
is still studied by present-day scholars. Because it stands
outside the Church tradition, the book presents a different perspective on the nature of the soul that is of
historical interest. Josephus reports that during the
times of Jesus, the Pharisees taught a belief in angels,
spirits and the migration of the soul into other bodies.

The Edgar Cayce readings say that in the New
Testament, on occasion, when the word "resurrection"
is used, it refers to reincarnation. Resurrection of the
body? Without the concept of reincarnation, we find
most contemporary theologians very embarrassed by
the reference in the New Testament to the resurrection
of the body. The passages in the Bible seem to be
referring specifically to a *physical* resurrection. This is
difficult for the scientifically oriented contemporary Christian theologian to handle.

When we talk with people who are interested in
the Bible about the concept of reincarnation, some feel
that because the *word* "reincarnation" is not there, the
teaching is not there. So they say, "No, it is contrary to
all the teachings." It is especially interesting to talk
with the literalist to see what he is going to say regarding certain literal references. For example, when we
quote Jesus as having said, "You must be born again,"
He was not talking literally about being born again, He
was talking about the spiritual rebirth. That literal
statement has to be qualified. But, when the writer of
Hebrews says, ". . . it is appointed unto men once to
die, but after this the judgment" (Hebrews 9:27) that is
to be taken literally.

Can we find references to reincarnation in the

Bible? Yes, and one of the most interesting of these is about John the Baptist as a reincarnation of Elijah. For background, I Kings 18:17-40 tells us that Elijah challenged 450 priests to a confrontation between their god, Baal, and his God. When their sacrifice to Baal failed, Elijah mocked the priests and, after his sacrifice succeeded, had them slain.

The coming of Elijah the prophet as promised by God is the last passage of the Old Testament (Malachi 4:5). Later, in the New Testament, Jesus, speaking at length about John, says, "For all the prophets and the law prophesied until John. And if ye will receive it, this is Elias, which was for to come. He that hath ears to hear, let him hear." (Matthew 13:13-15) Again, "'I say unto you that Elias is come already'... Then the disciples understood that he spoke unto them of John the Baptist." (Matthew 17:12, 13) Here finally is confirmation of the sameness of Elijah, or Elias, and John.

Note how the law is fulfilled that says, "whatsoever a man soweth, that shall he also reap"; for John was mocked by the people of his day as Elijah mocked the priests of Baal. Jesus' teaching that "All they that take the sword shall perish with the sword" was demonstrated in the beheading not of Elijah, who had the priests slain, but of John in his later incarnation.

Typically, the literalist will say, "Well, when the prophecy in Malachi says, 'I will send you Elijah,' it just means that someone will come in the *spirit* of Elijah. It does not really mean Elijah himself will return in the body." Thus they explain the passage away. If we are interested in exact wording, Jesus says John the Baptist and Elijah were the same. "He who has ears to hear, let him hear."

Reincarnation, as a concept, implies previous existence. There is considerable commentary in the Bible about previous existence. For example, Galatians 1:15 (RSV) says, "When he who had set me apart before I was born and had called me through his grace..." This expression "set me apart before I was born," has a quality of preexistence which harkens back to Jeremiah 1:5, "The word of the Lord came unto me saying,

'Before I formed thee in the belly, I knew thee and before thou camest forth out of the womb, I sanctified thee and I ordained thee a prophet.'" Another preexistence reference is found in Ephesians 1:4, "According as he hath chosen us in him before the foundation of the world that we should be holy and without blame before him in love. Having predestinated us unto the adoption of children by Jesus Christ."

Another strong preexistence reference is found in Romans 8:23-30: "Whom did he foreknow, he also did predestinate to be conformed to the image of his Son." Whom did he foreknow from the foundation of the world? The Edgar Cayce readings say *all of us*. We were created as children of God, made in His image, and He destined us to be conformed to that image of perfection. It is not only in the Edgar Cayce readings, but clearly in the Bible itself that we learn that we were created in the image of God and it is our destiny to be conformed to that image. We were one with Him in the Garden of Eden, we went astray of our own choice and although the wages of sin is death, He in His love and grace has made it possible for us to continue to choose, to move back into that relationship which is the destiny of us all.

There are many religious questions to which many of us never get a satisfactory answer. One of the first questions you may have asked even as a child in Sunday School is: "Why is it, if we are all created equal, that things don't seem to start out that way? Why is it that people start off with such fantastically different circumstances?" And I would add, why is it that we do not look carefully at this law that says, "Whatsoever a man soweth, that shall he also reap"? It is difficult to get a proper attitude about this. Only with the preexistence concept that we were originally one with God, that we went astray of our own choice and that we are meeting only what we have built for ourselves, can we come to understand the seeming inequities of the circumstances of man's birth. But are we to think of these circumstances as punishment? No, but rather that a loving Father is allowing us to see the consequences of our choices so that we may more quickly choose to return to oneness with Him.

A difficult passage is in John 9. A question is raised about a man who was born blind and the disciples asked, "Who sinned, this man or his parents that he should be born blind?" Jesus answered, "Neither hath this man sinned, nor his parents: but that the works of God should be made manifest in him." Now Jesus is not saying that no one committed sin, for many other teachings make it clear that *all* have sinned and come short of the glory of God. He is saying, rather, "Let's not think of our difficult experiences in the earth as punishment for sin but rather as learning situations for soul growth through which the glory of God may be made manifest."

One of the main reasons we need the concept of reincarnation in Christianity is to get a sense that there is a just and loving God. This problem must have plagued the heart of many an evangelistic preacher. The Bible says, "God is not willing that any should perish." (II Peter 3:9) Of this, the readings say that nothing truer was ever spoken. We cannot find credible a concept of a loving Father God who would permit his children upon their entry into the world to be placed in insurmountable circumstances.

Both science and religion need the concept of reincarnation to resolve some of their deepest problems regarding the nature of man. There are both evidential facts and Biblical bases for working with this concept. If we will examine the facts, we will find them numerous and strong. If we will read the Bible with this concept in mind, it will open up many confusing passages and the Book will make much more sense. This concept will make the Gospel more meaningful as it leads us on the path toward the destiny of us all one day to be conformed to the image of that perfection in which we were created.

The Soul's Quest for Wholeness

Healing or Wholeness?

When we think of healing, we should think of wholeness; when we are seeking healing, we should be seeking wholeness. If we follow the text of the New Testament, we find that these two words are used synonymously: healing means "being made whole."

Consider this story of healing from the Bible. A man was waiting by the pool at Bethesda in order to step into it, but he did not have anyone to help him get into the water. The Master came up to him and said, *not* "Would you like to be healed?" but "Would you like to be made whole?" That phrase, "being made whole," is reiterated throughout the Bible. Later, when Jesus saw the man again in the Temple, He said, "Behold, thou art made whole."

As we reflect on our condition, we find that we are not whole—none of us is whole. If we seem to be well physically, we may not be completely well mentally or emotionally. We are not whole as a people, as a nation, or as a world. Whether our diseases be of body, of mind, of family, of finances, of work, of productivity, of worth, of meaningfulness, or of fulfillment, there is always an unseen, vaguely felt, dimly perceived lack of wholeness of the soul that stands behind all disorders. It is the sickness of the soul which is the true reality, and our diseases and disorders are only symptomatic manifestations of it.

The Nature of the Soul

What is the soul? the Edgar Cayce readings give a great deal of exciting information on the soul, the destiny of the soul, the promise of the soul. A 16-year-old boy asked about the soul and received this answer:

What then ... is a soul? What does it look like? What is its plane of experience or activity? How may ye find one? It may not be separated in a material world from its own place of abode in the body-physical, yet the soul looks through the eyes of the body—it handles with the emotions of the sense of touch—it may be aware through the factors in every sense, and thus add to its body as much as the food of the material world has made for a growing physical body in which the soul may and does indeed dwell in its passage or activity in any individual phase of an experience in the earth. 487-17

A 35-year-old woman was told:

Know that ye *are* a soul, and do not merely attain to one; for the spiritual activity is of the Creative Force and thus is eternal. 2283-1

Another asked, "What is the soul of a body?" and received this reply:

That which the Maker gave to every entity or individual in the beginning, and which is seeking the home or place of the Maker. 3744-2

Several excerpts on the nature of the soul follow:

The soul is an individual, individuality, that may grow to be one with, or separate from, the whole. 5749-3

Man, in his former state, or natural state, or permanent consciousness, *is* soul. Hence, in the begin-

ning all were souls of that creation, with the body as of
the Creator—of the spirit forces that make manifest in
using same in the various phases or experiences of
consciousness for the activity.   262-89

Soul is that which is the gift of the Creator to be
the individuality that must present itself before the
Throne for judgment in its experiences through activities in whatsoever realm it, the soul, may find
itself . . . soul and spirit has no bounds save that it, the
soul, has builded or made for itself in respects to that
it has had the association or connection with as re-
specting its activity . . .   275-39

When there is the thought or the activity of the
body in any particular environ, this very activity makes
for the impressions upon the soul. For, the soul is that
body which lives on into infinity, and is the companion
of the particular body only in a particular or individual
experience.   416-2

These are some of the insights from the readings
about the reality of the soul.

The Nature of the Quest

As we think about the quest of the soul and its
experiences, we regularly find ourselves using analogies. One of these "quest" analogies is that of a pilgrimage. Frequently occurring in spiritual and sacred literature, this concept of the pilgrimage is used to depict
the soul's quest. The movement of Israel from bondage
in Egypt, to the wanderings in the wilderness, and
eventual entrance into the Promised Land is an illustration of this kind of pilgrimage—from bondage or death
to salvation and life. Many books, such as Bunyan's
Pilgrim's Progress, have dealt with this theme. Poets
work with this analogy, as Robert Browning's "Paracelsus,"
in which Paracelsus seeks for the truth and finds that
the "imprisoned splendour . . . takes no rise from outward things" but is found *within*.

The Master used such an analogy in the story of
the Prodigal Son, the archetypal pilgrimage of the soul.
Like the prodigal, each of us in the beginning was with
our Father but we went astray of our own choice. When
conditions in our lives today become worse and worse,
we finally come to ourselves and say, "I will arise and
return to the Father."

Sometimes the quest is depicted as an achieve-
ment, something to be acquired. The Holy Grail is an
example; or the parables of the Master speaking of the
Kingdom being like a field with buried treasure, or a
pearl of great price that might be obtained if one sold
all one's worldly possessions. There is an extraordinary
story which combines the acquisition/pilgrimage
theme. An elaboration of the parable of the Prodigal
Son, this apocryphal scripture is entitled "The Hymn
of the Soul." Let us consider just the beginning
lines:

When I was a little child,
And dwelling in my kingdom in my Father's
    house,
And in the wealth and the glories
Of my nurturers had my pleasure,
From the East, our home,
My parents, having equipped me, sent me
    forth.
And of the wealth of our treasury
They had already tied up for me a load.
Large it was, yet light,
So that I might bear it unaided—
Gold and Silver of Gazzak the Great,
And rubies of India,
And agates from the land of Kushan,
And they girded me with adamant
Which can crush iron.
And they took off from me the bright robe,
Which in their love they had wrought for me,
And my purple toga,
Which was measured and woven to my stature
And they made a compact with me,

And wrote it in my heart that it should not be
    forgotten:
"If thou goest down into Egypt,
And bringest the one pearl,
Which is in the midst of the sea
Hard by the loud-breathing serpent,
Then shalt thou put on thy bright robe
And thy toga, which is laid over it,
And with thy brother, our next in rank,
Thou shalt be heir in our kingdom."

The story continues: he went to Egypt and fell in with
friends who taught him their ways. He forgot what he
was about. He forgot the pearl. He forgot his heritage.
Finally, his parents sent him a message by a special
courier to help him remember who he was. He came to
himself, went to the dragon, got the pearl and returned
to receive the inheritance which was his.

    The journey of which we speak, of course, is not an
external physical one.

    Several years ago, a group of us made a tour
around the world. We went to the holy places in
England, to the Holy Land, to the Ganges in India,
among others. When I returned, I gave a talk entitled
"On Holy Places." I tried to build up the holy places as
beautifully as I could, and then commented on what it
was really like to be there. On one occasion we crossed
at the head of the river Ganges, the holiest place in all
India, to visit the Maharishi in his ashram and to talk
with him about meditation. As we returned across the
river, we were met by at least a dozen lepers, beggars
and others who were deformed and hideous in their
appearance. So the Ganges, with its great tradition of
healing waters (in which, it is reported, no bacteria can
survive), did not "feel" so holy. Lourdes, Glastonbury
Cathedral, the Ganges, the Holy Land, or some geo-
graphical location—is that what the soul is seeking? No,
these places are frequently so disappointing.

    Is it a person, a teacher, whom we seek in our
quest? Many people feel they must find a relationship
with a living master or a guru. We are told that on our

own we can make it only to the foothills; to climb the mountain, we must have a guru. So the soul's quest may seem to be to find that master or teacher. In earlier days, an audience with the Pope was for some a tremendous experience. Nowadays, with the enthusiasm for Eastern teachings, we hear that having a darshan with a holy man can raise one's consciousness. Many report having had such an experience.

Or is the journey one of becoming a channel for a spirit-being from another plane? Is it meeting a particular person who might, in reincarnation terms, be called one's soul mate? Seeking for a special person, whether mate, guru or entity from another dimension, may also be disappointing.

A few years ago a Buddhist priest from New Delhi named Bhanti visited the A.R.E. He was the President of the World Federation of Buddhist Monks. Someone asked him about the holy men in India. A wistful expression crossed his face and he said, "Well, one hopes, but when one looks closely..." He said no more, but it was clear that his experience in India, seeking holy men, had not led him to a fulfilling discovery.

For some, it seems, the quest is for a procedure or form—if we could just discover the proper technique for meditation, for example. Some say, "This is it. Just meditate by this technique, and this is all you need." Some take a more scientific approach: becoming "clear" of hang-ups through some instrumentation or mechanical means. Others would recommend participation in a ritual, ordinance, sacrament or initiation. Perhaps the soul's quest is to experience some process. Is it psychoanalysis? Or Rolfing? In spite of the signs of spiritual awakening, success is still the great American standard. Is success the way to achieve the ultimate quest of the soul? Is it a pill? LSD or peyote? Vitamin E or B-17? What is the nature of this quest?

How Long Is the Journey?

Some say, if we believe we will be saved. The truth of this may involve a longer journey than we care to imagine. The Edgar Cayce readings say that mankind has been in the earth plane at least 10 million years. This length of time is unimaginable to us. If we were to allow an inch to represent 100 years—near the maximum for a human life—20 inches would represent the time since Jesus. Six feet would represent more than 7,000 years or all of known history. The length of a football field, 100 yards, would then represent 360,000 years, and the lengths of three football fields would represent one million years. By this comparison, allowing one inch to represent 100 years, 30 football fields or nearly two miles would represent 10 million years. Many of us as souls sojourning in the earth plane have been here for that length of time! Thus the psalmist's query, "How long, O Lord, how long?"

How can we conceive of the magnitude of the gift of life, the heights from which we have fallen, and the endless duration of our present quest? How many A.R.E. or Theosophical Society lectures have we sat through? How many sermons have we heard in this incarnation? How many hellfire-and-damnation sermons did we tremble through in early America? How many Masses and Catholic services, in this soul's quest, might we have attended through successive incarnations in Europe? How many times have we fallen prostrate in Islamic prayer? How many times did we spin the prayer wheel chanting "OM" in our efforts to overcome successive incarnations? How many sticks of incense might we have burned in ancient India? How many of us might have attended a sermon given by Jesus or Guatama the Buddha? How many of us were challenged and threatened and exhorted by the Hebrew prophets, such as Elijah?

In our soul's quest for wholeness, how many pigeons did we sacrifice, how many lambs, how many bullocks? How many miles did we wander in the wilderness? How many years did we labor in servitude in

Egypt? How many bricks did we make during those years of captivity? How many months did we labor in the construction of the pyramids? In ancient Africa, the South Pacific, early America, how many drums did we beat, dances did we dance, and ceremonies did we conduct, in this quest of the soul to awaken consciousness? How many human sacrifices have we made to appease the gods? Long before that, how many Atlantean civilizations did we experience—periods of 20 to 40 or even 100,000 years? And even before that, in Lemuria? How many civilizatt̔ons rose and fell and rose and fell again? How many Lemurian inundations might there have been, for us to have gone back 10 million years?

Thus, in our soul's quest for wholeness, just think, imagine and ponder on how much we have done in these 10 million years in our search to be whole. In what untold array of things have we participated in this great quest? The Edgar Cayce readings say that the preparation of the work for the souls of men has gone down through thousands and millions of years, for hundreds and thousands of years yet to come. How many times in these 10 million years have our souls been quickened? How many times have we wondered, "Isn't there something more, isn't there a reality behind the great mystery of this experience in the earth plane?"

There is a story about an Indian chela, a student, walking with his guru along a seashore and observing the white, chalky cliffs. At dusk, with the pink light of the sunset reflecting on them, the student said, "Oh Master, let us walk here again tomorrow evening." And the Master said, "Do you wish to walk here again tomorrow? I tell you, the chalk of these cliffs is made of the very bones of your previous incarnations." The magnitude of time, in human terms, of the soul's quest is incomprehensible!

Where, Who and What?

Two things I would like to share with you regarding this journey. First, there are some considerations about *proximity*. Anyone who has done any journeying at all knows that it is more satisfying to return home than it was to get to the destination. The teaching that we have received is that the ground on which we stand is holy ground. The principle is, that the place where we are now is the right place—not just geographically, but with respect to the people with whom we have to deal, the jobs, the families and the talents that are ours. This is the place, the place where we are right now. As far as the place is concerned, the kingdom is within us. One of the strongest and last warnings of the Master was, "In the last days, there will be many who will say, 'He's over here, he's over there.'" And the warning is, "Go not out." In the soul's quest, that which we seek is not outside that we should go to another place to find it! Nor should our search be for a person to accompany us. The Master's promise is, "I will not leave you comfortless. I am with you always, to the end of the age." The promise is of His abiding presence.

Our second consideration is the process. It is simple enough! We are to love God and our neighbor. The readings say, "All you have to do is what you know to do now"; "Only the little things count"; "It is just in being kind"; "My strength is sufficient for thee." It is all so simple. So why the problem for 10 million years? Obviously, there is something about it that we have not wanted to learn. We have underestimated the magnitude of it. When we read the Bible, we find that the Master was reviled and persecuted. It is a message which is repulsive to us. It is a message that makes us so anxious and angry that we yell, "Blasphemy!" His promise to us is the same as for Himself: if we begin this quest, we will be reviled and persecuted. Which of us can claim these promises—to feel blessed when we are reviled and persecuted in His name?

We must re-examine this story very carefully to see why He was rejected and despised, and why He was said to have been so blasphemous, and why He said, "I have come to bring a sword, not peace, and to separate brother from brother and parents from children."

I would like to make one suggestion about why we have such difficulty in this quest for healing and wholeness.

An extraordinary reading (5749-14) was given for Tom Sugrue when he was writing *There Is a River*. Sugrue asked the reason for creation—it was God's desire for companionship—and whether man was supposed to have become involved in the earth. He was told that the earth was for the soul's experiencing and not necessarily for tenancy. So we were not supposed to have made homes here nor to have remained here so long.

Questions were also asked about the mission of the Master: "Is it correct that His was a voluntary mission of One who was already perfected and returned to God, having accomplished His oneness in other planes and systems?" Yes! the reading answered. Also included is that statement about the Christ Consciousness being the awareness within each soul, imprinted in pattern upon the mind and waiting to be awakened by the will, of the soul's oneness with God.

The Heart of the Problem

After receiving a number of answers, Sugrue finally asked: "Is there any other advice which may be given to this entity at this time in the preparation of these chapters?" The answer:

> Hold fast to that ideal, and using Him ever as the Ideal. And hold up that *necessity* for each to meet the same problems. And *do not* attempt to shed or to surpass or go around the cross. *This* is that upon which each and every soul *must* look and know it is to be borne in self *with* Him.   5749-14

This idea of the cross was taught even before the crucifixion of Jesus—not just in the teachings of the letters of the New Testament, but in the teachings of the Master himself. ". . . he that taketh not his cross, and followeth after me is not worthy of me." (Matthew 10:38) All of us are familiar with the story of the rich young ruler who asked Jesus what he must do to gain the kingdom of heaven. Jesus replied, "You know the commandments" and He listed some of them, to which the rich young ruler responded, "I have kept all of these from my childhood." Jesus said, "One thing thou lackest: go thy way, sell whatsoever thou hast, and give to the poor, and thou shalt have treasure in heaven: and come, *take up the cross* and follow me." (Mark 10:21)

In another account we are told: "'The Son of man must suffer many things, and be rejected of the elders and chief priests and scribes, and be slain, and raised the third day.' And he said to them all: 'If any man will come after me, let him deny himself, and take up his cross daily, and follow me. For whosoever will save his life shall lose it: but whoever will lose his life for my sake, the same shall save it.'" (Luke 9:22-24)

Now, that's the challenge: whoever would save his life must lose it. That is the mystery! That is the principle we have not wanted to buy! This is a hard saying. Who can hear it? All of us see the beauty of it, the simplicity of it, and the promise of it. But who can not only drink of this cup but also rejoice in it?

The readings say that He joked on the way to the cross, that He was light of heart and in good spirits. As He carried the cross on the way to His death, He gave other people encouragement. We have built too cheap a notion of heaven and thus have rejected it. We cannot get a sense of rejoicing about the completion of an incarnation: the meeting of pain, the meeting of a challenge, the meeting of disease, or the meeting of a catastrophe or a difficulty in our lives or in our families. We are not rejoicing in all of these because we are not sensing the requirements of them, the beauty of them and the promise behind them. "Do not attempt to . . . go around the cross."

As we think about healing, and look to its promises, we hear of instantaneous cures; we hear about the promises of instant mastery over pain and of the delay of death. We look to the present movement toward holistic healing as a measure of our soul's progress in its longing for wholeness. We get excited about the laying on of hands, and about work such as the Doctors McGarey are doing at the A.R.E. Clinic in researching the Edgar Cayce readings. We look forward with great anticipation to an alleviation of pain and of suffering, to the promise of a fuller life. Yet there is that one difficult thing that for millions of years we have not wanted to understand: that he who would save his life must lose it.

The *way*, then, is that manifested in the Creative Force through Jesus, the Christ, the Son; for He is the way, the truth, the light in which the body, the mind, the soul may find that security, that understanding, that comprehending of the oneness *of* the spiritual with the material that is manifested in an individual entity.

One finds the body, the mind, the soul of self as a counterpart of that an entity worships in the Godhead as Father, Son, and Holy Spirit.

So the body, mind and soul answer to that which is the source of health, of mind, of matter, in the experience of each entity.

To this entity these in the Godhead are one. So in the body they are one; body, mind, soul.

Body is temporal, mind is partially temporal and partially holy; the soul is eternal.

Just as the body then is the manifestation of the individual entity, the mind is the manifestation of the Son—both as an earthly experience and as an at-one-ment with the Father, the Whole.

So the soul is that which is eternal.

Thus does there come in the experience of each soul those problems in a material world of the constant warring of material or changing things, or earthly experience, with mental and spiritual or soul forces.

Remember rather the pattern as was manifested for thee in the Son; how that though He were the Son, yet learned He obedience through the things which He suffered.

He used, then, that which was necessary in the experience in the earth as periods of suffering, as periods of rejection, even by His own that He had called, that were His friends; not as stumbling stones but as stepping-stones to make for thee, for the world,

that access for each soul, for the closer relationship of
the Father, through the Son, to the children of men.

This is thy heritage, then; not as one that knows
not, but as one being reminded—put on the whole
armor. Fret not at those things that may appear to
hinder, but let that harmony as thou hast expressed, as
thou may express to others, be in such measure as to
bring—even as He—that hope, that light, that peace
which comes from the closer walk with Him day by
day.   2600-2

We are to use then "periods of suffering . . . periods
of rejection . . . not as stumbling stones but as stepping-
stones . . ." We must find and understand the beauty
and the promise of our *destiny* as children of God. We
are assured by the love of an all-merciful Father that we
are to return to Him and be made whole. Yet, on the
journey home, we must use apparent difficulties as
stepping-stones. With a positive attitude, we can follow
the pattern that was set for us by the Son Himself who
learned obedience through the things which He suffered.
What is it that must be crucified? The self, the rebellious self-will, the expectation that things will go our
way. How are these met day by day? Here a little, there
a little, by the willingness to relinquish self.

But this lower self can be repressed; it can be
pushed aside. It is far more dangerous lying hidden in
repression than up where we can see it. Only when it is
dead is it not dangerous. The symbol of the crucifixion
is the death of that lower self. Now, we are not told that
we will be crucified in the way of Jesus; but even before
that, He encouraged us to take up our cross daily and to
follow Him. When the lower self is indeed crucified in
obedience to His will, then we are assured of the
resurrection to new life, to wholeness, in our inheritance as joint heirs with Him in the Kingdom.

As we think of attunement for healing and reflect
on the soul's quest for wholeness, let us consider the
glory of that state from which we fell, the eons in which
we have been astray, and the promise and proximity of
the Way. But let us not too quickly forget to measure

the cost of the journey. Let us find some way in prayer and in the promise of His abiding presence to rejoice as He did in taking up the cross daily.

The Psychology of the Symbol Seven

The psychological is just one of a number of ways to approach the great literature and the sacred writings of the world. It is perhaps no more and no less valid than any other approach. However, in dealing with material of a clearly symbolic nature, it may be very helpful.

The writings in our Bible are to a very great extent symbolic in nature; consider the value placed by the writers on dreams, visions, parables, rituals and special numbers. The clearly symbolic nature of the number seven is an example of such material. From the "seven days" of the first chapters of Genesis to the reiterated sevens of the Revelation, this symbolic number is so seriously utilized in the Bible that any consideration whatever of its presence is certain to lead to the recognition of its potential for being profoundly significant.

It is quite clear *numerologically*, as contrasted with *psychologically*, that the "mystic seven" is an integration of the "mystic three" and the "mystic four."

In many times and among many peoples, three has been the number of Heaven, of the Spirit, of the Triune God. There is a Trinity in Hinduism as well as in Christianity and other religions. Likewise, four has been the number of the Earth, of materiality, the four seasons, the four directions, the four elements of the ancient Greeks and Hindus (Earth, Water, Fire and Air). hence, seven is the number expressing the sum of, or the integration of, heaven and earth.

An especially noteworthy instance of the Biblical use of the number seven is seen in the seven golden candlesticks of the tabernacle worship. The height of a man, and being made of one piece of pure gold, the *menorah* stood in the holy place into which no outside light was allowed to enter. Thus it was the dominant (preparatory?) stimulus pattern confronting the priest. The afterimage of it must have continued to burn in his eyes as he entered the Holy of Holies where he was to meet God face to face.

The psychologist is not so much interested in understanding symbols, but rather in understanding man. In a psychological consideration of symbols, the basic concern is the relationship, or identity, of the external referent, the symbol, and the internal referent, within the individual. The term, projection, is used to conceptualize behavior in which the person experiences the referent as being external when it is in fact internal. Physicists are becoming aware of the importance of this principle. Heisenberg has said that when examining nature and the universe, instead of looking for and finding objective qualities, "Man encounters himself." (Jung, p. 307, *Man and His Symbols*) The nocturnal dream is an example of behavior in which the persons or animals or symbols seen in the dream are experienced as being external to the dreamer but which in fact depict physiological and psychological events taking place inside the person. If this same principle of projection is applied to understanding religious experiences or visions or symbols, remarkable insights may be obtained about the nature of man and the meaning of his experience.

However, man is very resistant to developing an awareness that what he experiences or expects to have an external referent has in fact an internal referent. Not only is man resistant to this insight but he sometimes becomes quite anxious when confronted with it. ·

Thus the Master was not understood in saying, when you would worship—that is, when you would confront God—you will not find him in the holy mountain or in the temple but within, in spirit. (John 4:20-24) He was not understood when He said, "He that hath seen me hath seen the Father." (John 14:9) He was not understood in His approach, which I am here calling the psychological approach, when He pointed out repeatedly the relationship between the external referent, which was the symbolic, and the internal referent, which was the real, psychologically, phenomenologically and experientially. Not only was He not understood but He raised the anxiety level of His listeners to the point of open hostility against Him. The repression of these insights is a motivated one in us all because such insights challenge us to recognize our divine heritage and cosmic responsibilities.

The crucial question of the whole discussion is this: is the almost universal valuing of seven as a sacred number an arbitrary and spurious superstition or does the number have a referent? And the psychological question is: does that referent have its locus or at least its representation in man? Is the symbol seven the externalized or projected referent for a psychological or physiological process or structure within man? Has man used this symbol because it reflects something within himself? And, as the presence of the seven of the candlesticks in the tabernacle worship suggests, is it specifically related to attuning man to an awareness of the presence of God?

The writer of Hebrews said that the tabernacle was a "shadow of heavenly things" (Hebrews 8:5), that the first tabernacle was "a figure for the time then present," (Hebrews 9:9) ". . . but Christ being come an high priest of good things to come, by a greater and far more perfect tabernacle, not made with hands . . ." (Hebrews 9:11) "For Christ is not entered into the Holy places made with hands which are the _figures_ of the _true_ . . ." (Hebrews 9:24)

What or where is the _true_?

The writer of Corinthians says, "Know ye not that ye are the temple of God and that the Spirit of God dwelleth in you?" (I Cor. 3:16)

If the body is the temple or tabernacle, what is the referent within the body for the seven candlesticks having something to do with worship?

Simply posing the question in this way leads the

student of comparative religion to a startling answer: for thousands of years, those accomplished in the practice of Kundalini Yoga or Raja Yoga, the highest form of Eastern meditation, have taught that in deep meditation the yogin becomes aware of and senses the activity of seven spiritual centers within himself—four in the body and three in the neck and head. Many writers have associated these centers with the seven major endocrine glands. These are clearly emotional centers: consider the relationship of the adrenals to anger or the sex glands to the strength of the sexual drive.

With avoidance of all interpretation, explanation, and evaluation, the phenomenology of deep meditation involves a feeling of awareness of centers within the body, the visualizations of which have led to their being referred to as lotuses or as *chakras*. The lotuses are seen as flowers with differing numbers of petals. The word *chakra* is Sanskrit and it signifies a wheel. The fact that experiencing the activity of these centers may be accompanied by the visualization of wheels leads to an interpretation of Ezekiel's vision of the wheels.

Ezekiel says, ". . . the heavens were opened and I saw visions of God . . . and the hand of the Lord was there upon [me] . . . And I looked and behold, a whirlwind came out of the north, a great cloud and a fire infolding itself, and a brightness was about it, and out of the midst thereof . . . came the likeness of four living creatures. And this was their appearance; they had the likeness of a man . . . As for the likeness of their faces, they four had the face of a man, and the face of a lion . . . (and) the face of an ox . . . (and) the face of an eagle . . . Now as I beheld the living creatures, behold one wheel upon the earth by the living creatures . . . and when the living creatures were lifted up from the earth, the wheels were lifted up. Whithersoever the spirit was to go, they went . . . for the spirit of the living creatures was in the wheels." (Selections from Ezekiel 1)

In yogic terms, the wheels Ezekiel saw would represent the visual experiences which would accompany an opening of the spiritual centers or *chakras* or wheels within the body.

Accompanying Zechariah's vision of the candlestick of gold with seven lamps, was a vision of four chariots. In the first chariot were red horses, in the second black horses, in the third white horses, and in the fourth grizzled and bay horses.

And the angel said to Zechariah, "These are the four spirits of the heavens which go forth from standing before the Lord of all the earth." (Zechariah 6:5) Here the vision of wheels is implied by the vision of chariots.

The vision of four beasts, by Ezekiel, and the vision of four colored horses, by Zechariah, are both experienced by John in the Revelation, a description of his own spiritual experience.

Granting the relationships suggested up to this point, it would then follow that the referents for the symbol of the candlestick with seven lamps are the seven spiritual centers. The seven churches of Asia, addressed by John, have as their referents the seven emotional centers, the endocrine glands, within the temple of the body. The faults and virtues of the churches are the emotional faults and the spiritual virtues potential to every man.

Jesus said, "I have yet many things to say unto you, but ye cannot bear them now." (John 16:12) Carl Jung has said, "By a symbol I do not mean an allegory or a sign, but an image that describes in the best possible way the dimly discerned nature of the spirit. A symbol does not define or explain: it points beyond itself to a meaning that is darkly divined yet still beyond our grasp, and cannot be adequately expressed in familiar words of our language." (*Collected Works of Carl Jung*, Vol. 8, p. 336)

Is it possible that by attributing a psychological, that is, a personal meaning to the symbol seven that we can gain an entry into the Revelation which will prove it to be personally applicable and revealing? "Blessed is he that readeth, and they that hear the words of this prophecy, and keep those things which are written therein: for the time *is* at hand." (Revelation 1:3) Can we hear what the Spirit is saying to the churches without a psychological approach, or will our reluctance to adopt such an approach keep us from understanding the Revelation of John as well as from experiencing our own revelation?

For example, if we do not understand that the four beasts of Ezekiel's and John's revelations are archetypical of the four baser emotions within ourselves, we may fail to notice the admonition from John that the four beasts must bow down before there can be spiritual attunement; that is, before the revelation can proceed. Ours is a time in which the four beasts within are clamoring for ascendance. Consider the church of Ephesus. The city of Ephesus was known for its worship of the multibreasted Diana, a fertility cult for which the calf is an archetypically appropriate symbol.

The fault of the Church of Ephesus was that it had left its first love (Rev. 2:4), and more than once in the Old Testament when men turned from the love of God they made for themselves golden calves to bow down before. Man has in many times and places worshiped the bull, the cow, the calf—the external symbol for the internal referent, the sexual emotions. Are we not in our own time dangerously close to sexual cultism? Speaking individually, is this beast within bowing down so that the revelation may proceed?

The angel said to the Church of Ephesus: "Remember therefore from whence thou art fallen, and repent, and do the first works; or else I will come unto thee quickly, and I will remove thy candlestick out of his place, except thou repent. But . . . to him that overcometh will I give to eat of the tree of life, which is in the midst of the paradise of God." (Rev. 2:5, 7)

Thus the warnings and the promises go, "He that hath an ear, let him hear what the Spirit saith unto the church . . ." (Rev. 2:7)

Or, consider the third church, the referent for which may be the adrenals and the solar plexus whose potential for power is appropriately symbolized by the lion. Is ours not an age in which the symbol of the power of the great cats is being used to motivate the sale of cars, tires, gasoline, breakfast cereals, clothing, etc.? The talk of power in every context of our life indicates the way in which this beast within wants to rise up and rule our lives rather than bow before the throne.

The eagle is the symbol for the fourth church whose virtue is love but whose fault is fornication. The symbol of the bird whether eagle or vulture, or hawk or dove or mother hen, is used to illustrate *concern*. This emotion may lead to love or it may lead to fornication, and ours is a time when this emotion, also this beast within, wants to rise up and rule the earth rather than bow before the throne.

We have contrasted the four of the earth with the three of heaven but the Revelation does not speak of three spirits of heaven but rather of the seven lamps of fire burning before the throne, which are the seven *Spirits of God*. (Rev. 4:5) Here we have a suggestion about the nature of God as well as man. Not one in three but one in seven, in which the four of the earth and the three of heaven are integrated in one. The writer of Exodus was told to make the candlestick of one piece of gold and he was cautioned, ". . . look that thou make them after their pattern which was showed thee in the mount." (Exodus 25:40)

The branches of the candlestick suggest one of the names of Christ. Isaiah says, "In that day shall the branch of the Lord be beautiful and glorious . . ." (Isaiah 4:2) and, ". . . there shall come forth a rod out of the stem of Jesse and a Branch shall grow out of his roots . . ." (Isaiah 11:1) Zechariah says, "Behold the man whose name is the Branch; and he shall grow up out of his place, and he shall build the temple of the Lord . . ." (Zechariah 6:12) Again Zechariah says, "Hear now, O Joshua the High Priest, thou, and thy fellow that sit before thee: for they are men wondered at: for, behold, I will bring forth my servant the Branch. For behold the stone that I have laid before Joshua: upon one stone shall be seven eyes: behold, I will engrave the graving thereof, saith the Lord of hosts . . ." (Zechariah 3:8)

Thus in Christ we find oneness: oneness of heaven and earth, oneness of the three and the four, oneness in the sacred and the secular.

I wonder if a satisfactory paraphrase of the first lines of Genesis might be, "In the beginning God *became* heaven and earth"—suggesting a panentheistic* integration of the best aspects of the concepts of transcendence and immanence.

This concept gives recognition to the dynamic bipolar tension which came out of the first creative act, but eliminates from the outset the ever-troublesome problem of dualism.

In Christ, as John saw him walking in the midst of the candlesticks, we find the possibility of oneness in the universe as well as oneness in the motivational and emotional forces within ourselves; however, the four are needed as well as the three. Just as the seven colors of the spectrum are needed in the right balance to obtain white light, so the full spectrum of our emotional potentials in the right balance is needed for us to manifest the white light of the transfigured Christ in the earth.

---

*Panentheism is the view that attempts to reconcile the insights of *pantheism* and of *deism*. Pantheism identifies God and the world taken as a whole while deism insists that God and the world are separate entities. Panentheism argues that the world is included in God's being much as cells are included in a larger organism, although the world does not exhaust God's being or creativity. God has all of finite being as *part* of His being and experience but transcends it. This view necessarily rejects the view of God's complete independence from the world.

Meditation: The Hub of Healing

Meditation is not only the hub of healing, but should be the hub of our lives. Yet, it may be the most talked about and least practiced of the activities recommended by every spiritual teacher. As we seek to understand healing, let us re-examine meditation to seek a deeper understanding of what it is and what it does.

Of the many strange stories that come out of the Edgar Cayce readings, the most unusual are contained in the life readings, as in the following complete reading regarding Achilles—whom we ordinarily think of as being a mythological figure. The young man of Jewish background requesting the reading was told that there had in fact been a man named Achilles and that he himself had been that person in a previous incarnation. He asked for a check reading to get more specific details about this life. He was told:

In the entrance into the earth's plane in that of, or called, Achilles, we find it was in the period of earthly existences when conditions were accentuated along certain lines. The entity then was as the male offspring and entered in with the beauties of the rustic nature of the time and place, near Athenia or Athens, and was raised to manhood, or young manhood, in and about the Mount, and given all advantages in the exercises and games and learning of the day, with the beauties of that in that day as could be obtained by one that was raised for the special purpose of entering into the political, social and other conditions of day and age. Soon learned that of the soldier with spear, bow and axe, with an armor as prepared by the mother of the body, and given all the benefits of the aristocrats of the age, given exceptional abilities and applied same in the moral, physical, development of the body. One, then, beautiful of stature, physical, mind and of the expressing of same. Soon drawn in early manhood into the political situations surrounding the conditions of the country, coming then as a companion to many of the leaders in that day when there were personal combats in every phase of the physical prowess of the body. The entity showing the exceptional abilities of the environments under which the body had been developed in the day when this, the development of physical prowess, was studied and given the greater extent of attention. In personal combats often the body was successful and was called the leader of the army and group, or the personal representative of the armies of the entity in the reign of those in charge of same at time.

In the social and moral life, we find the entity one showing development in mental abilities. One showing development in moral conditions, as was shown in the relation to captives as were taken by the armies and distributed, the favorites to the favorite of the army. In the personal combats we find the exceptional abilities in mental forces also shown. The entity then departed the life in personal combat, wounded in the heel, from which gangrene set in in body and became blood poison to the system. In the day we find much written concerning this entity, and there are given many abilities that are only written in the form of the day and age, as is written of many who show their abilities in a manner that is developing in earth plane toward the spiritual forces to which all strive.

Departing then with only the forces as of not being able to meet the needs of physical suffering under the conditions which came to same. Only erring then in that manner. Hence in the present plane the necessity of being able to meet these conditions that

would seem to overwhelm the entity, but necessity of, as has been given, Be still—and listen to the voice from within. 900-63

Here is one who was given all of the opportunities imaginable at the time, receiving a relatively minor injury. He erred only in his lack of the ability to be still and tune in to that healing force that could and should have come to him at that time. And this was his lesson to be learned in the present incarnation—that he must be still.

All of us must indeed some day learn to meditate, because all of us must some day come to be one with the One Force. And the practice of meditation, of course, is the practice of the movement toward that oneness. However, it seems that we have a way of coming upon an insight, realizing it—like turning on a lightbulb and finding suddenly that the light is there, and then turning it off again—forgetting the new insight and returning to the former darkness. So it is regarding what we know about meditation.

The healing power of meditation is well known to us. Carl Simonton, M.D., is a physician who has developed a treatment for cancer combining meditation with radiation therapy. In *Psychiatry and Mysticism*, edited by Stanley Dean, M.D., Dr. Simonton reported on his research in an article, "The Role of Mind in Cancer Therapy." In this article, he related the story of a 35-year-old woman who had a carcinoma of the uterus. She had been previously examined by a gynecologist and had already developed a very bad infection—a serious sign of a downhill course. Upon reexamination several weeks later it was found that the tumor had decreased in volume by at least 50%. Astounded, Dr. Simonton asked her for an explanation. The woman replied that she had been drinking four glasses of grape juice daily, as she had heard that this would help tumors. Later, as Dr. Simonton relates, "When I was getting ready to begin her treatment, I started to explain to her what I wanted her to do regarding her relaxation and imagery. She looked at me and said, 'My, that sounds like meditation!' I said that it certainly could be considered meditation, and asked her why she made this statement. Her answer was that approximately a year previously she had begun reading Edgar Cayce's work and had started meditating on a regular basis, and it had changed her life. I then asked if she had been meditating regarding her tumor, to which she answered that indeed she had been, and she felt that that was why the tumor had gone down. When I asked her why she had told me it was the grape juice, she said she was afraid to tell me that she thought it was the meditation for fear I would ridicule her for doing it, and she felt very strongly about it.

"Well, we continued with her treatments and had an excellent response. We were very excited to have found someone meditating on her own and having a tumor go away without any treatment, only the meditation, in a way that made sense to me."

Why don't we pursue these insights about meditation and healing with greater energy, greater commitment, and greater verve? Perhaps we have not understood or reflected fully enough upon all that is involved in the practice of meditation. Let us review, then, some of what we know about meditation.

In the study of biology one finds that the human body is fantastically adapted to life on the earth. It is a special instrument for coping with and expressing mastery and creativity in the earth plane. It is also another special kind of instrument. We may think of it as God's special solution to a problem—His children as spiritual beings cutting themselves off from the awareness of His nature. Because we had placed ourselves, lodged ourselves, gotten stuck—as it were—in a three-dimensional plane, it became necessary to develop an instrument that could manifest in such a plane and yet one which had the capability for the awareness of oneness with the Infinite. In the development of such an instrument, there had to be within it the potentials for all of its consciousness to be aware of its oneness with the Divine. There had to be the sensory potentiality for experiencing that awareness in consciousness. Therefore if we have built within ourselves the capability of experiencing an awareness of oneness with the Whole, we can think of the body as a miniature model of the universe. Insofar as we were—and are—children of God, it became His task to develop a way, a special instrument, for our becoming aware of our oneness with Him. This is one way of understanding the principle that we are made in His image.

Part of our problem, then, becomes one of working with these two extraordinary potentials of this instrument. Since much of our life of adapting in the earth plane requires attention to external stimuli for survival, we have developed a fantastically sensitive reporting system. If the construction of a room is ¼ inch higher on one end than on the other, we are aware of it. Because we have such a fantastic sensory system, we sometimes become uneasy when we see something out of place. If a foe were after us, it would have extraordinary survival value for us to be so sensitive. But when there are no threats, the sensitivity remains and we become worriers. We think that we are specially endowed because we are so aware of what can go wrong; we think we are especially astute because we can observe (particularly in our neighbor) such an array of items that have a potential for being corrected. Then, we get a sense that we are fairly good observers because of such awarenesses. Since there is survival value in our becoming aware of minute changes in the environment, we keep orienting outward and thinking that attention to the input of external stimuli is required for us to survive! This may become so much so, that we have great difficulty even in falling asleep—and certainly in setting aside a few minutes in which we would reverse that process, as in meditation.

Borrowing from communication theory, we will consider what is called the "signal noise ratio." In our orientation toward the external environment, we define any stimulus coming through the senses as the "signal," and anything coming from within us as "noise." If we are confronted with a decision and we have facts from outside ourselves upon which to base the decision, we are more likely to be concerned with those facts than with some internal awareness. To the voice within we say, "That is the noise. I've got to concern myself with the signal," that is, the externally originating information.

The practice of meditation is taking just a few minutes a day and saying to those sources of external input, "Be still." We move the functioning of our instrument away from adapting to the earth plane and toward an attuning to the Infinite. We must be convinced that the physical body is made in such a very special way that it is optimally constructed for an attunement with the Infinite. This involves the physical, the mental and the spiritual; the physiological correlates of these are, respectively, the sensory system, the autonomic nervous system, and the endocrine system.

The autonomic nervous system relates particularly to the mental body; it is the mediator between the external senses and the attunement of the seven endocrine centers, which are the gathering or rallying centers for spiritual energy as well as the sensitive centers for the attunement. Meditation may be thought of as a reorganization of the nervous system, responding to the imaginative forces of the mind. The physiology of this is, in part, a movement away from sympathetic to parasympathetic activity. The sympathetic is that activity in which Achilles apparently was so strong that he could master external threats. The sympathetic is, of course, the fight or flight system; but the parasympathetic is that system which is responsible for the quiet periods of the body: regeneration, recuperation, rest, reproduction, assimilation—all that would go with healing.

In meditation, the parasympathetic system becomes dominant over the sympathetic. The imaginative forces of the mind awaken within the body its recuperative function and quiet the survival function.

As beginning meditation teachers will tell you, becoming aware of one's own breathing is the one entry whereby one gains immediate conscious control over the autonomic nervous system. Using a simple breathing exercise (such as inhaling, saying, "I am," exhaling, saying, "Relaxed") can put us in touch with the mediating autonomic nervous system; and immediately an integration and a reorientation of the systems of the body begin.

To pursue the physiology of that reorientation, we shall examine reading 281-24, which considers the laws of spiritual healing more in terms of physics than of physiology. The reading suggests that all healing at its finest level is a rebalancing of the atom's rotary forces. It is also a balancing of the energy system at the atomic level, which may be out of equilibrium in terms of being too active or not active enough. In Sister Justa Smith's biochemical research with the healer Estabany, the healer held trypsin, an enzyme material, which had been exposed to radiation. He enhanced the healing effect of the enzyme by his "laying on of hands." On one occasion, without telling Estabany, Sister Justa set up her experiment so that a decrease instead of an increase in energy would be required to bring about the desired effect. After he had held the materials, the photospectrographic analysis showed that the correction had been made. Evidently the "healing" was not just the adding of energy, but the correcting of the balance of atomic forces. If you have "healthy" atoms, then it follows that you will have healthy molecules, healthy cells, healthy tissues, healthy organs and a healthy body.

If we can get a sense of how the physics of correcting the balance of the atom works, we may also get a sense of how "magnetic" healing may truly be magnetic, and why there may indeed be instantaneous cures (such as the instantaneous removal of tumors reported by many spiritual healers). The occurrence of these healings may resemble the placing of a magnet over a field, an action which corrects the magnetic forces. All of us have had the experience of putting a magnet near a pin, a nail, or a hairpin, and discovering that the item involved becomes a magnet. If we have one aligned system—a person in whom the atoms are balanced, for example— and if we place it close to another system, we can get an alignment in the second system. In the Cayce readings we are told that when we fully raise this healing energy through ourselves, we become like a magnet. Perhaps this analogy from the readings could be fairly literal.

In the experiment cited previously, Sister Justa reported that Estabany's healing effects could also be attained by a magnetic field. Now, the magnetic field about the earth plane is .5 of a gauss. It was found that a 13,000-gauss magnetic field was required to get the same healing effect in the injured trypsin as when Estabany held it. We may also think of the human body as an energy system, such as a battery. Imagine placing a wrench across the poles in an automobile battery. The wrench would no doubt melt. But what if we attached the wires of an FM radio across those poles? We'd immediately have symphonic music, but we'd also have picked up, tuned-in on and amplified waves coming from a great distance, analogous to clairvoyance. The difference between the wrench and the radio is not the energy but the circuitry through which the energy flows. It is the same energy. We move from a wrench to a radio, and the difference is merely the patterning through which the energy flows.

We are like that battery. The Hindus call one pole of this battery the root chakra from which the kundalini energy arises; the other end is called Brahma's crevice through which that force enters the head. These centers, similar to the two poles of a battery, are the entry points of the Holy Spirit about whom Christians speak. One force but with two poles, so that there might be a flow.

When we meditate, that which determines the experiences we have is the circuitry through which this energy flows when raised. What determines and selects the circuitry? The imaginative forces and the motivation. The quality of motivation and what is done with the mind are what select the channels through which energy flows. When there is a motivational quality that has a correspondence to the integrated functioning of the whole system, then we may say that we are in full attunement and in the highest state of meditation. What kind of motivation is likely to select the optimum circuitry out of this whole complex of motivational potentials? We know that the motivation of anger may select the response of the adrenal system; the motivation of sex may select the response of the gonad system. We know there are other endocrine systems to which we may not have attached as direct an emotion or motivation. We hear about the heart being related to love. But even though the adrenals and gonads have specific emotional and motivational correlates, it has not really occurred to us that the rest of the endocrine system might also.

How would it be if the whole of the endocrine system were working in concert? Think of the seven centers as a seven-piece band with all of the instruments playing together. It is not as though one plays and the others are quiet, but we can bring one forward playing in solo, or two forward playing together while the others are in the background. This is the complex functioning of the endocrine system. What brings one forward to play solo? The *imaginative* system, setting the purpose, the *ideals,* the *motivational* system. If we dwell upon anger or resentment, we call forth the trumpet, a call to battle; then the adrenal fight-and-flight system takes over and plays louder than any of the rest. We do not get the harmony that might come from pulling the other systems forward.

What is meditation? Meditation is putting the leadership of that band in its proper place. The problem is that these motivational and emotional systems that refer to survival in the earth plane are responsible for protecting us in an emergency.

They have the stronger override potential, like the military general who says: "The country is in a state of emergency. I've got to take charge." And they can indeed take charge of the whole system. In the Edgar Cayce readings on the Revelation, in which he interprets the seven churches as relating to these centers, it is said that the seventh church—the Church of Laodicea—which would be the pituitary, has the fault of being lukewarm. It is good that the pituitary does not respond like the adrenals; then perhaps we would have people growing a foot taller overnight, what with the extraordinary power of its secretions when released. How do we activate this higher center? The Edgar Cayce readings state that if one were acted upon by the pituitary alone for seven years, he could become either a light to the world or a Frankenstein monster. The activation can be made even though the motivation is not necessarily the highest.

In *The Secret of the Golden Flower,* we are told: "In the square inch field of the square foot house, life can be regulated. The square foot house is the face. The square inch field in the face: what could that be other than the heavenly heart?" This square inch field of the square foot house is the pituitary and is called "the heavenly heart."

In the pituitary and the hypothalamus (the great control center in the brain located just above the pituitary), we have the centers where life can be regulated. Then the text asks: "How can you move the heavenly heart? If you can be absolutely quiet, then the heavenly heart will spontaneously manifest itself."

Only as the utmost quietness is attained may the whole body be regulated. The text likens this state to a king sitting on his throne—having already established the fundamental rules of order—while the menservants and maidservants go quietly about performing their proper work. When this higher integrative physiological system is in charge, then all of the activities in the human body perform their proper function.

Meditation is reorganizing the nervous systems; in particular, the parasympathetic is moved into a more dominant position. The flow of energy that results leads to the balancing of the atomic forces. Meditation is becoming a magnet, integrating the whole force field about us; it is raising the kundalini to meet the Holy Spirit. In a special case it involves also the teaching that mind is the builder, by enabling us to dwell upon that which we want to become, to dwell upon the attribute or quality of motivation that we wish to awaken. That that we dwell upon, that that we feed our minds upon, that do we become. Further, that which the mind dwells upon is supplied to the physical body and to the soul.

Psychologically, what may happen in meditation is a reorganization of the hierarchy of response systems. Many of us know about S-R (Stimulus-Response) psychology. A stimulus leads to a certain response, but its refinement lies in that a stimulus may lead to an array of responses. If you give a dog a bone and then take it away from him, he may bite you or he may growl. It is improbable that he will wag his tail, but he might. There are several possibilities of response. Meditation is reorganizing the hierarchy of the response system. Let us examine how this may work. It is in terms of a principle that *The Secret of the Golden Flower* calls "making a medicine of the illness." Most people feel that they cannot meditate because they cannot quiet the mind. They do not understand that the process of quieting is an important part of the meditation procedure, and is a part of learning and experiencing meditation.

Meditation is directing the mind with the imaginative forces awakened by a high ideal (such as, "Not my will, but Thine, O Lord"), trying to awaken a response and, as the mind drifts off, bringing it back and reawakening the ideal. We usually complain when the mind drifts off. However, we should not deny it nor complain about it but acknowledge what has happened. To "make a medicine of the illness," the following may be used as an illustration: As I meditate in the morning, my mind drifts off to an afternoon job interview about which I am concerned. So first, I acknowledge the fact of my mind drifting. Second, I invite the Spirit of Christ (or God) to stand between me and the situation. I say, "Lord, this is important. I know it can be handled only in Your Presence. I cannot handle it, but I know You can." And third, I say, "Because this is important, it's all the more reason why I need to take these few moments to become centered." Then I let the importance of the interview be the remotivator for orientation toward becoming attuned and centered. So quieting the mind, then, involves the releasing of that concern into His Power, the reorientation toward the task at hand, attuning, and then the reawakening of the spirit with the affirmation.

How does this relate to reorganizing the response hierarchy? In an ongoing practice of meditation, we begin to put our concerns into relationship with the divine and release the concern to Him. We begin to make a different response to each stimulus. For example, let's say that every Thursday afternoon you have an appointment with Joe, with whom you are having difficulties. In your meditation during the week, when your mind drifts off to your concern with Joe, you try to sense the presence of the Christ in this relationship. In your next meeting with him, instead of making the usual negative responses, you will find yourself responding to him with a more loving attitude. Why? You have relinquished your anxiety. You know that there is another Power working in the relationship. You are more loving and Joe responds by being more cooperative. In the practice of meditation over the days and weeks, your mind will drift off so many times that there will be no major condition in your life that has not been put in a different perspective in relation to the Divine. Here you are "making a medicine of the illness." The drifting off becomes a way of reordering the response hierarchy, a way of reorganizing the motivational system in respect to every specific event or person with which you have to deal. As we pray repeatedly for others, we prepare ourselves to respond to them more lovingly.

The readings advise filling each center with the ideal when meditating. I work with this literally. First, I go through the Lord's Prayer as it relates to those seven centers; then I go back through it and try to sense *life* and *light* and *love* or the Christ Spirit as filling each of those seven centers. As we fill those centers with life and light and love, we can reorganize the whole motivational system.

Meditation is, in Jungian terms, moving toward the realization of the archetype of the Self, and thus toward the individuation or actualization of our full potential.

There is written within us a pattern of perfection. The Old Testament writers say that this law is not far from us; it is written in our hearts and minds. Meditation is choosing that law as the ideal and dwelling upon it. Psalm 1 says that he who meditates day and night on the law of the Lord is blessed and that everything he does will prosper.

Dwelling on the law of the Lord is dwelling on the awareness of the pattern of the Self. Meditation, as it relates to the attunement of the centers—also symbolized by the climbing of Jacob's ladder—is entering into the Holy of Holies. In prayer, we address One above; in meditation we meet on common ground, going into the Holy of Holies and meeting Him face to face. Meditation is choosing life instead of death. It is the practice of the great commandment to love God with all our hearts and minds and souls. There is no more direct way of indicating our love for another than in wanting to be present with that one. The practice of meditation is saying, "I want to be present with the Divine." It is the great practice of the great commandment, the love of God.

Meditation is listening to the still small voice. Remember that the prophet in the Old Testament found out that God was not in the whirlwind, not in the lightning, not in the thunder nor in the earthquake, nor in any of the mighty ravings of nature, but in the still small voice. Psychologically, the ravings of nature are the ravings that may come from within ourselves. Earthquakes and fires are within us. There are all sorts of internal experiences that we might receive from within. But the Divine is not in those fantastic experiences, but in the still small voice. Psalm 46 says, "Be still and know." We wonder how can we know by being still? We have yet to learn a great deal from the Buddhists about the concept of the void, which is not empty.

Meditation is the practice of the immanence of the Divine; it is saying that the Divine can manifest in the earth plane. Like the woman at the well to whom Jesus said, "If you had known to whom you were talking, you would have asked of him and he would have given you

living water," meditation is the drinking of the water of
life. It is partaking of that of which Jesus spoke when
He said, "I have meat you know not of."

The readings say that actual creation is taking place
in meditation. A possible understanding of this statement is that, at the subatomic level, energy is moving
into manifestation and becoming "particle-ized."

In addition, meditation is the great turning-about
within the deepest seat of consciousness, which the
Buddha recognized as the only miracle of all the siddhis.
It is the practice of the awareness of the prodigal who
came to himself and said, "I will arise, and go to my
Father." We are all prodigals. By meditating, we are
turning about and saying, "I will return." Jesus said,
"Behold, I stand at the door and knock." Meditation is
opening the door and inviting Him to enter. The readings say, "Why entertain others when He is so nigh?"
Yet they also say, "He will not be the uninvited guest."
There's a gentle pressure, a knocking of that force to
flow through us, but it must be *invited* and *allowed* to
flow through. This requires intention and time.

In the Bible we are told that we are created in the
image of God. In some passages of the New Testament
we are told that we are destined to be conformed to
that image. (Rom. 8:29) Meditation is the practice of
moving toward our destiny, because it is the movement
toward conformity to that image of the Divine implanted
in us; it is therefore fulfilling destiny.

Meditation is accepting grace and allowing the
force of life and love to flow through us. It is creative
and, therefore, corrective of those patterns that we call
karmic. In this sense, it is turning stumbling blocks into
stepping-stones because, as we meditate, we put everything in relation to God. We see Him in every relationship and we sense every opportunity, every confrontation in life as a way of drawing closer to Him, to place
our faith more fully in Him. Meditation is partaking of
the bread and wine. As the Spirit flows through us, we
have the true Eucharist and a literal transubstantiation.

In the Revelation of John, meditation is the bowing
down of the four beasts, telling the four lower motivational

systems of sustenance, self-gratification, self-preservation and self-propagation to be still and quiet. As the four beasts and the twenty-four elders bow down, the senses and the activity of the brain must bow down to the higher direction. We are told in the Revelation of the 144,000 souls, and we may think of these as symbolizing perfect patterns within, that meditation is inviting the 144,000 to manifest in our bodies. The readings say the number also represents the effacing of that strange fearsome pattern of the beast numbered 666. If we are marked with that number, meditation is the erasing of that pattern and the replacing of it with another higher pattern—the mark of the Lamb. We are a book with seven seals; meditation is the practice of the opening of those seals. Remember, though, that in the Revelation John saw that no one in heaven or on earth was worthy to open those seals. But the Lamb came and He was worthy to open them. Thus the instructions regarding meditation are that the opening of those seals must come from the Spirit and not by some intervention of our own.

Finally, we may think of meditation insofar as it is an invitation to His presence, as the most meaningful and personally applicable understanding of the Second Coming. And as the Revelation closes, we are told that the Spirit and the Bride say, "Come. And whosoever will, let him take the water of life freely." Meditation is the drinking of that water of life.

Guides, Gurus and
the Gospel

In this century, we have seen an extraordinary development of two approaches to spiritual growth. One approach—receiving spiritual guidance through a medium—has a more solid base than ever before because of developments in the field of psychical research. The other approach—receiving teachings from holy men, living masters or gurus—has a new basis for acceptance because of a new and widespread interest in examining religious and philosophic teachings different from our own. For some, these new approaches have presented a challenge, even a conflict, between the new insights being offered and the older understanding of the message and warnings of the Gospel.

One of the strongest warnings in the teachings of Jesus is that in the last days, "Many false prophets shall arise and shall deceive man." (Matthew 24:11) We are cautioned, "Go not forth...believe it not." Yet Jesus Himself was, in some terms, a guru and a living Master and He, in turn, sent forth disciples to heal and teach in His name. The Bible warns against false prophets; yet it is filled with instances of the manifestations of the same gifts as those of some of today's psychics and healers. In the experience of some, Edgar Cayce has been a true messenger from God; however, to the minds of others, he has been a false prophet. Thus, a critical problem arises for anyone seeking to be on the spiritual path. How are we to discern the spirits, that is, between those who might be guides or gurus sent to us by God and those who might be false prophets?

In 1951, my wife, who was then my girlfriend, was attending Stanford University while I was going to electronics school. She and I were walking one day in the hills behind Stanford and, as we crossed a little bridge, we simultaneously had one of those experiences that is referred to technically as *déjà vu,* the feeling that we had been there before. As a result of that experience, she thought I would be interested in reading the book, *There Is a River.* I had been reading the Bible, Freud's *Psychoanalysis* and Rhine's book, *The Reach of the Mind.* Somehow I knew all these divergent views must come together. After reading *There Is a River,* everything fell into place for me.

Throughout these two decades, I have tried to get a closer, in-depth understanding of the Edgar Cayce readings. The more I study them, the more deeply I sense the convergence and unity of all things. A source of direction, reassurance, stimulation, optimism and purpose in life seems to grow out of these readings. It is very dismaying, therefore, to hear intelligent people asking why Cayce is not allowed to die or be left alone since there are now so many good sensitives around, giving readings. "Why dig up the Edgar Cayce thing?" they question. This kind of remark is dismaying because it reflects no understanding of what the work is about.

A young man who was very close to the work of Edgar Cayce received more than 400 readings. He was told that he had been, and could become, a most extraordinary person; but even this man failed to grasp and retain the deep sense and purpose of these readings. He was told that in a previous life, as Achilles, he was almost perfect; he could, if he wanted to, rejuvenate his body, become a sensitive exceeding Cayce himself, and integrate the religions of the world. He received his first reading around the age of 30 and by the time of his last reading at age 35, he had made a fortune. In the late '20s, he helped Cayce build a hospital and establish a university that was given the promise of changing the consciousness of the world. But, alas, some difficulties developed. Though Cayce was extraordinarily accurate in his psychic readings, a few of his diagnoses did not exactly fit with what a physician had reported. This great young man began to doubt and turned to another alleged psychic. Misunderstandings developed, the stock market crashed, and he lost everything—even though he was forewarned to get out, not only by his own dreams but by the readings. Following these events came a separation from the work.

We find, then, that some who have been closest to this information, most excited about and most committed to it, have drifted away from it for reasons that do not seem to be directly related to the quality and content of the information itself. Sometimes, it seems that those who moved away had not been fully clear about some of the major premises and so turned to other sources.

In our country and time, so many voices call us to so many sources of information. It is not surprising that many are confused about where to turn for help. Once we become interested in the implications that psychical research has on understanding man's spiritual nature, many doors open and we are confronted by such an array of questions that the complexity of it all may dazzle us.

We need, then, to get some basic premises straight. The apostle Paul said that he could talk in terms of philosophy, mysteries and a variety of things; but, "I have not to know anything among you save Jesus Christ and Him crucified." (I Cor. 2:2) We can see the insight he had when he decided to stick to the basic principles. However, he also said, "I have fed you with milk and not with meat." (I Cor. 3:2) ". . . and we have many things to say, and hard to be uttered, seeing ye are dull of hearing. For when for the time ye ought to be teachers, ye have need that one teach you again which be the first principles of the oracles of God." (Hebrews 5:11-12)

Let us, then, in examining experiences with guides and gurus, keep in mind some basic premises and move toward a more mature diet. One of the occurrences with which we may be confronted is a relationship or experience with an entity from the spirit plane. A young man in Los Angeles was going to a "development class." At a conference on the West Coast, a friend insisted I speak with the young man immediately because she felt it was an emergency. Technically, he was on the verge of moving into psychotic disorganization. Besides extreme physical reactions and anxiety, he also had peculiar sensations in his body which he experienced as forces operating on him from the other side. His eyes were dilated, and he was having somatic delusions. All the organs in his body were doing unusual things. He wanted and needed help. He told me he had come to see me reluctantly that evening because he was missing his "development class." He intended to go on to the class as soon as he talked with me.

In his "development class" he had opened a door, and was becoming aware of entities on the other side. Some of them wanted to speak through him, one of whom was his grandfather. He was very excited about this breakthrough. I asked him, "If your grandfather were alive today and living 30 miles away, would you go over and talk with him?" He replied, "Well, that depends . . . No!" He would not have gone out of his way to visit his grandfather if he were alive, but now that he was on the other side that was a different story. He did not intend to give up this development class because to him it was exciting and stimulating. All he wanted was help to get rid of the impulses that were overwhelming him. It seemed to me that there was a direct relationship between the "development" of the mediumship and the occurrence of the serious symptoms. This process was beginning to destroy his life, causing him to lose touch with himself completely.

Some people are convinced that just by dying— graduating from earth living—an entity necessarily moves to a higher plane of consciousness.

On another occasion, a man told me of an unusual experience. He said he could at will do astral projection, moving in consciousness outside of his body. In a dream, he found himself moving to a new level where he was met by someone who gave his name. He had not heard of this man before but subsequently discovered that this person had written many books about soul travel or astral projection. While the dreamer was in that state of consciousness, the author took him through some experiences in that new dimension. At one point, the dreamer saw some distance away a great area radiating light. Some people were there, singing beautifully, and he wanted very much to go over to see them. His self-appointed guide, though, said he could not go because, "That's Jesus and His bunch over there." This seemed to me to have been most unfortunate. Had he followed his own inclination rather than that of his guide, he might have had an extraordinary experience.

The Edgar Cayce readings say that this kind of communication with others in the spirit plane is possible. Once, as he was giving a reading, Edgar Cayce began talking as though he were involved in a one-sided telephone conversation in which the people in the room heard only his side. After the reading, those in the room asked him what had happened and Cayce told them that, had they wanted to, they could have heard both sides of the conversation provided they would attune themselves to such a realm during the experience. These readings confirm that it is possible to be in touch with people on the other side and hear them.

We should note, however, his suggestions concerning the different kinds of experiences. He told one person to study all phases of psychic phenomena but not automatic writing because it would lead to detrimental rather than beneficial channels. Someone asked if automatic writing could be developed; Cayce replied that anyone could do it. Later, the same person asked how to develop it. Cayce told that person to practice by sitting alone with a pencil and paper and letting the guide come in and direct. However, he mentioned that this guide should always be questioned. Another asked if her inspirational writings were to be relied upon, were they coming from a high source, or should she not at all cultivate this form of guidance. The answer was:

We would *not* from here counsel *anyone* to be guided by influences from without for the *kingdom* is from within!

If these come as inspirational writings from within, and not as guidance from others—that is different!
1602-1

Another inquired, "Do I have any direct guidance from invisible helpers?" The answer indicated:

. . . ever the guardian angel stands before the throne of God—for each individual. **3189-3**

Another person was told:

The sojourn of a soul-entity other than in materiality often influences or bears weight with individuals within the material plane—as an odor, a scent, an emotion, a wave, a wind upon the activities.

Such are termed or called by some guardian angels, or influences that would promote activities for weal or for woe. **538-59**

On one occasion, a being named Hillaliel, an archangel, presented itself through Edgar Cayce and offered to give a series of discourses. Considerable debate was generated among the group, some wanting to hear what the guide had to say and others feeling it would not be in accord with their higher purpose. Later, after the group made the decision not to seek information through this being, the higher source of the readings assured them that they had made the right choice.

The apostle Paul said, "Though I speak with the tongues of men and of angels and have not love, I am nothing." Can one speak with the tongues of angels and have not love? It was said in the reading that Hillaliel was "one who from the beginning has been a leader of the heavenly host, who has defied Ariel, who has made the ways that have been heavy—but as the means for the *understanding*." (254-83)

One of the most extraordinary sets of readings we have in the files is the one Cayce gave on Eileen Garrett and one she in turn gave Cayce through her guide, Uvani. In terms of accuracy, Uvani mentioned an incarnation of Cayce that he had not given himself in his life readings. The Cayce source was asked if this were really true, and the source confirmed the accuracy of that life but did not see any reason for Cayce to know of it. With respect to the question of the presence of outside influences, the readings gave support to the notion that these influences existed but suggested that we consider the purpose for our becoming channels: is it a personal thing or is it that we may manifest the Fatherhood of God, the brotherhood of man, or the universal Christ Consciousness in the lives and affairs of others?

In talking about those on the other side, it should again be stressed:

. . . **do not consider for a moment (for this might be carried on to an indefinite end) that an individual soul-entity passing from an earth plane as a Catholic, a Methodist, an Episcopalian, is something else because he is dead! He's only a dead Episcopalian, Catholic or Methodist. And such personalities and their attempts are the same; only that *ideal*! For all are under the law of God equal.** 254-92

When our bodies die, we still take our orientations with us. Eileen Garrett's guide, Uvani, in identifying himself says, "I am an Arab." He does not say, "I was an Arab," nor "I had an incarnation as an Arab." He says, "I *am* an Arab." To illustrate the point, we might question his objectivity in commenting on questions relating to Israel.

Of course, instances in the Bible speak of communication with entities on the other side. In his time, King Saul had all those with familiar spirits killed. One

called the Witch of Endor escaped death. When Saul
was in trouble, he sought out this woman who was a
medium. Saul wanted to talk to the deceased Samuel
regarding his problems. The Biblical story states that
Samuel appeared. Saul said, "I am in distress... God
has turned away from me and answers me no more,
either by prophets or by dreams; therefore, I have
summoned you to tell me what I shall do." And Samuel
said, "Why then do you ask me, since the Lord has
turned from you and become your enemy?" (I Samuel
28:15-16) If we have turned away from the Divine
within, how shall we hear Him through another?

Someone requested, "Will you explain for the entity just how the abilities in the writings may be
developed?" And the Cayce readings said:

**By applying self in first opening self for those
influences that may aid in guiding that as may be put
into expression. For, as given, *seek beyond that veil
that is also seeking aid*... [Author's italics]   497-1**

Notice this especially: "Seek beyond that veil...
rather to the realm where teachers, ministers, advisors
would come..." (4971) From whom are those on the
other side going to learn or seek aid?

**... seek beyond that veil that is also seeking
aid... surrounding self with that influence where there
is the consciousness of the Christ—whether ye call
Him by some other name, it must be from the Throne
of Grace.   497-1**

Now, what about guides? Yes, there are numerous
entities in the spirit plane—those who would possess,
those who would try to teach, those who would be
archangels or the higher sources, and guardian angels.
The readings say that countless entities inhabit the
spirit plane who, not taking cognizance of their present
state, still want to have a say in the affairs of the earth.

We are our brother's keeper and we are interested
in helping others. Not only might we receive help from

the other side but, on occasion, we might help them. It works both ways. Cayce did a fantastic ministry in counseling with confused souls in the spirit plane. He could talk with them and help them find their way.

Yes, we can help each other, but what is our ideal? Is that the way we want to seek? Do we really want that as an ideal? Do we want a contact or an on-going relationship with a specific person on the other side? Let us hold this question in mind while we consider another.

Many of the same claims describing the ways that guides help are also made for gurus, living masters in the earth plane. Numbers of people today are looking for a guru. Even though they are told "When a student is ready, the master will appear," they feel that a search for him is required in order to indicate their readiness. Recently, a young man, who was on his way to India, wanted some instruction on how to find a holy man there. I asked about his understanding of having a guru and suggested several books, including the biography of Milarepa.

This great Tibetan yogi spent a lifetime meditating. In the beginning of his search, he found a living master, a guru, named Marpa who, as a test, gave him several tasks involving building houses. Marpa took him up on a high plateau where there were some extremely heavy boulders. After instructions were given, Milarepa worked and worked, but when he was about half finished, Marpa came by and said, "You were not listening. I did not say I wanted it there. I wanted it over here and I wanted a crescent." Next, the instructions called for a triangular house in another place. Then a third time, Marpa came along and said, "That's ridiculous; whoever heard of that! I want a square house in this place." So he made him tear it down again and rebuild it. Very strict obedience is one of the major factors in the guru-chela (student) relationship. Marpa was testing Milarepa's obedience. I asked the young man, "Do you intend, when you find your guru, to be obedient to his every command, no matter how strange it may seem to be?" He said, "No, I'm my own director, my own guide." He only wanted a holy man to lift him in consciousness, but was not willing to be fully obedient to the commands of such a teacher.

Raynor Johnson, author of many books dealing with metaphysical aspects of life, is a beautiful and delightful person. On a lecture tour of the United States in the early 1970s, he spoke to many people of the necessity of having a living master. We asked him, "Could we publish some of your lectures?" He said, "Well, I'll have to consult my master." He was very excited about a new idea for a book and eager to get back to Australia so he could check with his master to see if it would be all right to write it. That's obedience! For all who have questioned this teaching, saying that Christ was their Master, I have challenged them to be as obedient to the commands of Christ as Dr. Johnson was to his teacher. What would happen if we would be equally obedient to the best that we know in ourselves for even a few days? We would probably find a tremendous change in our lives.

A young man from New York was very excited about a certain guru whom he wanted me to visit. He said, "Just being in his presence will raise your consciousness." There are many great, well-developed persons; there are highly psychic people; highly sensitive people; very holy men. On a trip to India, we saw some of these men with very high and unique consciousnesses. Is that our ideal? To find someone to whom we could be obedient and in whom we would put our trust? Some speak of the guru as taking over the person's karma. Do you want to put your trust in that person?

One of the most interesting of all the readings speaking of the Christ says, "*He* is thy *karma*, if ye put thy trust *wholly* in Him!" (2067-2) Karma is memory; it is activating, energizing those patterns that we have built into our memory. Rather than awakening such, we may awaken that pattern written inside us of the Christ, so that it can become our karma. One person inquired: "What leader or teacher could guide body along the path?" The response:

Him! In Him! Along the ways that were given by
Him! Be satisfied with nothing less than He as thy
guide, by day and by night! Let ever that mind be in
thee: *"If His presence abides not with me day by day,
may I not be lifted up!"* 452-6

Not only are there Eastern gurus, but there is a
variety of teachings, books, writings and organizations
that would seek our loyalty. A 38-year-old woman asked:
"Is Unity the answer to my nerves?" She was told:

It should be the *Christ* as the answer, not Unity or
any cult. But know this in self: As given of old, think
not who will descend from heaven to bring a message
that ye may know, or who would come from over the
seas; for Lo it is within thine own heart, thine own
mind. Then remember as He has given, "I go to
prepare a place that where I am there ye may be
also—if ye love me, ye will keep my commandments
and I and the Father will come and abide with thee."
Then what is thine answer? Put thy hand in His. For
who healeth all thy diseases? Who supplieth thee with
life, with food, with shelter? His force, His love, His
confidence in thee. Forsake Him not. 3247-1

A 23-year-old man queried, "On which of the
Masters of Wisdom should I meditate for spiritual guidance?" And the reading said, "There's only one Master."
(3545-1) A 56-year-old woman wanted to know, "What
should be my next step with some associates—especially
in the Arcane School?" She was told:

This can best be answered in self, when those
suggestions here indicated are within self.
This is not meant to be as a finding of fault—with
any; but rather that self *knows* within self those that
are the best channels, the best manners in which
teachings, ministerings, may be *simplified* in the experiences of men; that they may reach them *where* they
are! God is God of *all*; not just a chosen few who may

appear to have more intellectual or physical or mental abilities than others...

So, in thine own experience in the offices as a teacher, consider these—and be wise, in Him. 2402-2

Yet, in all our turning within, we must understand the body to be the place of contact with the One God. Meditate upon this reading: "Those who look only to the God within may become idol worshipers, for the experience that is of thy concept is what one does about that concept." "Our spirit bears witness with His Spirit" is a great teaching about the Divine within. The readings discussed the faults and virtues of various countries.

What is the sin of India? Self, and [leave] the "ish" off—just self. 3976-29

This beautiful teaching indicates we may lose our way if we do not identify the Divine within, relate it to the Divine without, then apply this concept in action.

Here is an example of a woman who was uplifted by her reading and invited to humility at the same time: "Am I the chosen channel for the enlargement of Methodism in more vital, Christian relationships?" He answered:

A channel. Few would choose to be *the* channel. For *the* channel must be in *Him*. But as a representative of Him in such a service, *well* chosen. Well to magnify, not any cult or denomination—for Christ is Lord of all. Through that organization, well—but magnify the Christ, *not* the method. 2574-1

Edgar Cayce never requested anyone to leave his or her church or religious organization. He wanted everyone to think of those organizations as opportunities for service. The teacher should be the spirit within; the organization is the context in which we can serve.

These readings suggest there is only one Master.

There has also come a teacher who was bold enough to declare Himself as the Son of the living God.   **357-13**

Some people want to know what is so special about Jesus. Are there not many other living masters? For some reason, it makes us anxious talking about the divinity of Jesus. When He said, "I and the Father are One," someone wanted to stone him. It was to them blasphemous. What was His response? He said, "Your own law says you are gods." He did not say, "I am God and you have got to come to me," but instead, "I am of God and you are my brothers. I have come to tell you and show you by my life who *you* are." So he stated, "It is not I but the Father in me." Jesus, the Christ, was the Teacher bold enough to declare Himself the Son of the living God.

He set no rules of appetite. He set no rules of ethics, other than "As ye would that men should do to you, do ye even so to them," and to know "Inasmuch as ye do it unto the least of these, thy brethren, ye do it unto thy maker." He declared that the kingdom of heaven is within each individual entity's consciousness . . . to be aware of—through meditating upon the fact that God is the Father of every soul . . .
What, then, is this as an ideal?   **357-13**

To love God with all our hearts and our neighbor as ourselves. Each of us will find our true self in applying what we know of the ways of the Father and the Christ and by seeing Him in the hearts and lives of others. It is not so much self-development but rather developing the Christ Consciousness in self. What is the Christ Consciousness? Being selfless, allowing Him to have His way with us, to direct our lives and to guide us in our daily activities.

A 42-year-old woman asked this question, "How may I bring about greater emotional stability?" And the answer was:

As the body-mind entertains and enters into the raising of the kundalini influence through the body, surround self with the light of the Christ Consciousness— by thought, by word of mouth, by impressing it upon self. And in that light there may be never any harm to self or to the emotions of the body, or any fear of the mental and spiritual self being entertained or used by the dark influence.   2329-3

A 32-year-old man wanted to be recommended to a physician. The reading said, "The most physician needed is within self. The physician is the Christ Consciousness." (3384-1)

Another asked the question that summarizes all the questions we have had about guides and gurus. "Where can I get concrete guidance besides from the inner voice?" And he said:

Seek not other than that of His meeting thee within thine own temple. For beside Him there is none other. Know, as He gave, they that climb up some other way are robbers.

Then, listen—listen to that voice within. Prepare thyself, consecrate thyself, purify thy body, thy mind, in much the same manner as did those of old . . . And then, open thy heart and thy mind to those promises; surrounding thyself with the consciousness of the Christ love. And He stands and knocks. Will ye entertain Him? Then, do not entertain others.   2029-1

Perhaps we are asking, as one seeker did, which spiritual teacher would be the best for us. The answer: "Why not rather turn to Him that each of these would bring to thee . . ." (1299-1) Regularly those who ask their living master about Jesus are told that Jesus of Nazareth was the Master of masters.

Why not rather turn to Him that each of these would bring to thee—thyself? Begin with those promises He hath given. Read the 14th, 15th, 16th, and 17th chapters of John. *Know* that they are not to someone else but to thee! And why would you use other forces when He is so nigh?

For as He has given thee, "If it were not so I would have told you." And this means *you*!

For the Father hath promised and has given us a body, that is a temple of the living soul, which is that temple in which ye should meet Him day by day.

For as the pattern was given even in the mount of old, when ye turn to Him, He will direct thee. Why, O why, then, [turn] to any subordinate, when thy brother, thy Christ, thy Savior would speak with thee! 1299-1

We have been examining the kind of advice given in these readings.

Do not be satisfied with substitutes; for He will walk and talk with thee and ye will recognize Him in, "Fear not, it is I."   2405-1

The person who had just heard that, asked: "Will I contact my master in this lifetime?" He was told:

Read what has been given. For, He will walk and talk with thee; if ye seek to do His biddings. . . . 2405-1

Another asked, "What is the right road for me to take which I have not yet found?" The answer:

As indicated, first know *what is thy ideal!* There is none other. Let it be in the *spiritual* forces, *not* in the material. Seek to know *the Christ Consciousness.*
1167-2

When he says there is no other ideal, he is saying the ideal of the great commandment—to love God with all your heart and your neighbor as yourself. The ideal is others—not self. There is only one ideal.

Q-1. What should be the guiding principles of my life?

A-1. Jesus, the Christ—and *Him* crucified! 1456-1

... would that all would learn that He, the Christ Consciousness, is the Giver, the Maker, the Creator of the world and all that be therein! And ye are His ... He *is*, He *was*, He *ever will be* the expression, the *concrete* expression of *love* in the minds, the hearts, the souls of men ... He will guide thee, for He hath given His angels charge concerning those that seek to be a channel of blessing to their fellow man ...   696-3

This is the type of material received from these readings about guides and gurus. It is important we realize that we are not talking about organizations; we are not talking about philosophies; we are not talking about Eastern versus Western thought. Someone asked about this work and the teachings of Christ; the readings said:

... be ye all things to all men; thereby ye may save the more. For he that declares as a name, in a name, save in the universality of the Father, limits the ability of the seeker ...   254-85

If we know someone of a different background than ours and we require that he get out of his organization and into ours, or require him to stop calling God by one name and start calling Him by another—if we require our own ideas of other people we limit the abilities of the seeker. We are not talking about an organizational, doctrinal or a dogmatic movement. We are talking about the direct contact which every individual may make with the God within which is one with the God without—the Oneness of the Spirit within all men.

The Master, in giving one of his last sermons, warned about the latter days. Ours may indeed be the latter days. But the meaning of this message to the individual is far more important than any reference to macrocosmic events. Jesus said that in *our* last days of growth, as we move to an acceptance of these concepts, to an awareness of the reality of God and the spirit within, as *we* move into the latter days of our own development and consciousness—as Jesus did when He moved into the temptation in the wilderness—that we will meet a challenge, a temptation which is going to be difficult. Once we have gotten on the path and have begun to grow and work with these principles, then we should look out for this problem.

They are going to say Christ is over here, He is over there, come out here, go out there. And that last kind of temptation, that sense of, "I've got to find something out there that will give me the information, that will give me the healing, a contact that will pick me up when I'm low, something I can depend on," starts us seeking *out there*. That is going to be one of the last temptations. The readings say, "No greater psychic lived than Jesus of Nazareth." (2630-1) He could have ruled the world without raising a hand. Yet, He chose the way of love. That is all he asks us to do—to live in the spirit of love. There may be many ways that we would seek—"Isn't Buddhism just another way? Aren't they all different paths to the same goal?" For dramatic reasons, I would say, "No." There is only *one way*. And that is the life in the spirit. Spirit manifesting in and through the individual. The way is not Buddhism nor A.R.E. nor Christianity nor any of these organizations. Yes, there will always be a vessel, a structure through which the spirit expresses on the three-dimensional plane. But *the way* is the *action* of the spirit *through* the structure and not the structure itself. It is not the information—no matter how true or accurate it may be. *The way* is in the expression of the Spirit. What does God's Spirit manifested look like? In the life of love, you will recognize it.

Jesus' consciousness attained extraordinary awareness: He said, "I must go so that I can send you the Comforter." Now in His life we have a pattern of what love looks like manifested in the earth. The teaching in Deuteronomy 30 is: "Don't say who will go thereforth and bring it so that we may know it and do it; it is written in your heart." The same teaching is in Romans 10: "Don't say who will ascend into heaven or who will descend into the abyss, that is to bring the Christ up from the dead." It is written in your heart and your mind so that you may know it and do it.

Now here is the key and central thesis: as we turn within and attune to His Spirit seeking, He may send us to others—a druggist, a surgeon, a minister, a healer, a sensitive, a teacher. Remember after a healing He said, ". . . go and show thyself to the priest. . ." (Luke 5:14) and to "Go, wash in the pool of Siloam . . ." (John 9:7) As we seek the Spirit within, He directs us to the next step.

Why then do we continue to study, research and talk about the Edgar Cayce readings? They do not bear witness to themselves. These readings do not say, "Read the readings and believe in them." Although they say the Bible is the word of life, they do not say, "Believe in the Bible." Someone asked what is the best translation of the Bible and the readings said, "The nearest true version . . . is that ye apply of whatever version ye read, in your life." (2072-14) Edgar Cayce did not come to teach us to be Christians, or Jews, or worshipers of any religion, but to live in the spirit of love.

As we come to understand reincarnation and that we have experienced the earth plane for millions of years, we find that the situation of the soul of man is far more serious than we had imagined. Nevertheless, the *good news*, the *gospel*, is far bigger and better than we have ever imagined. We have let ourselves and our concepts be limited. We have, as the readings say, given others power over us.

Man is hedged about by beliefs, by cults, by schisms, by isms—yes. And those things have been created by man and he hath given them power in themselves to rule his days . . . For the spirit of truth and wisdom is mighty, and a bulwark of faith and hope to those that trust in Him . . . Thus hath He declared, as was given of Him who is the way, the truth and the light, the first, yea the whole of the commandment of the Lord is encompassed in this: "Thou shalt have no other god before me . . ."   **2454-4**

Now this is very important in relation to guides and gurus, great and helpful as they may be.

. . . "Thou shalt have no other god before me, neither in heaven or in earth, nor in things seen or unseen, but thou shalt love the Lord thy God with all thine heart, thine soul and thine body, and thy neighbor as thyself."

This, then, is the premise from which all judgments by the individual are to be drawn, knowing that the law of the Lord is perfect, it converteth the soul; knowing that the promise of the Christ is, "Lo, I am with thee always, even unto the end of the world."

He was in the beginning, He is the end. And as ye walk in the light of His promise, of His words, ye may know the way ye go. For His light shineth in the darkness and maketh the paths straight for those that seek His face.   2454-4

That Divine is near us; it is closer than even the hand. It is written within us. That is the source of all life. When we choose to accept His love and grace and to live in the Spirit, we have good news indeed!

Charisma and Kundalini

I would like to arrange a marriage. It may seem at first to be a very improbable match. I want to arrange a marriage between a serpent and a dove. The serpent is kundalini coiled three and one-half times, sleeping within each of us at the base of the spine. It is the Eastern symbol of the life force lying dormant within us. When raised in deep meditation, this energy becomes the enabler of the siddhis, the miraculous manifestations of the yogis. The dove is the Holy Spirit, descending upon the heads of those quickened by it as tongues of flame. This is the Western symbol of the life force in whom we live, move and have our being. When it comes to us, it brings charismatic power and healing, and transforms us to new life. But why speak of a marriage? Marriage is symbolic of a union, of a coming together to become one. Thus such a marriage would work toward an integrated and unified awakening of the creative and transformative energy which may flow through us.

The first premise from the Edgar Cayce readings is the oneness of all force. It is not so much that there is one God, but that there is *One*. God *is* One. To get a sense of the oneness, we are encouraged to study this principle of oneness for six months. For any question raised in our minds, we receive insight when we apply the principle of oneness to it. Yet problems arise when we see divergencies not only of religious orientations but more importantly in religious, mystical, and psychic experiences. We see and hear of such a divergent array of experiences from which come different teachings, schools, methods and techniques. We may have considerable difficulty in seeing the oneness behind all of these; but the concept of the oneness of all force should be that to which we return every time we have a question about seeming discrepancies.

Let us examine in detail two firsthand experiences from two extraordinary men of greatly divergent backgrounds. Let us reflect upon these experiences as illustrations of the problems that arise in our search for oneness.

We will look at the charismatic experience of Marcus Bach consequent to his fervent prayers, and we will look at the kundalini experience of Gopi Krishna, from India, consequent to his devout practice of meditation. Let us note especially the similarity between Bach's experience of the charisma of the Holy Spirit and Gopi Krishna's experience of raising the kundalini.

Marcus Bach is a great student of comparative religion and author of many books, including *The Inner Ecstasy*. He begins this book with a discussion of the day he spoke in tongues. His friend, Joseph, is chanting, praying fervently for Marcus' baptism. Marcus, meanwhile, is experiencing rending conflict—on the one hand clinging compulsively to rationality and yet longing desperately for purification. The more he realizes he shouldn't think, the more furiously thoughts race in. The more he realizes he *has* to let go, the tighter he holds on, until he feels the mounting tension will break him. Then "A strange thing was happening. I was feeling light, relaxed, trancelike. I was aware that my lips were moving and that I was mumbling incoherently. Something was using my vocal cords . . . 'Koina kara, lamani, mera!'

". . . the I that I thought I knew began moving out of range, moving into shadows, forced into retreat by an oncoming blob of light . . . An ecstatically pleasant, thrilling surge of passion swept through me as if the Holy Ghost, whatever it was, had finally found an entry . . .

". . . with a rush of gibberish welling up from deep inside me, I burst into hysterical laughter and weeping and sprawled to the floor in freedom and delight."

Now let us compare with this the kundalini experi-

ence Gopi Krishna reports in one of his books on the
subject, *Kundalini, the Evolutionary Energy*. During
regular meditation, he would sit for hours, facing the
east, and focus his attention on an imaginary lotus
crowning his head in radiant light.

One day in particularly intense meditation, he felt
an incredible and pleasing sensation stirring in the base
of his spine. As his attention went to it, it vanished.
Dismissing it as a trick of the mind, he returned to the
lotus. The feeling returned more intensely, his mind
was again drawn to it, and again it disappeared, leaving
him vexed and agitated. When he finally calmed and
settled into deep meditation for the third time, "Suddenly, with a roar like that of a waterfall, I felt a stream
of liquid light entering my brain through the spinal
cord.

". . . The illumination grew brighter and brighter . . .
and [I] felt myself slipping out of my body . . . I was now
all consciousness, without any outline . . . without any
feeling or sensation coming from the senses, immersed
in a sea of light simultaneously conscious and aware of
every point, spread out . . . in all directions without any
barrier or material obstruction. I was . . . no longer as I
knew myself to be . . . but a point, bathed in light and in
a state of exaltation and happiness impossible to describe."

The most striking similarities between the charismatic and the kundalini experience are, of course, the
experience of the light, the dissolution of the self,
intense exhilaration, and the realization of the extraordinary in what had happened. Here we have two
experiences of considerable similarity yet one is attributed
to the descent of the Holy Spirit and the other to the
raising of kundalini.

Afterwards, what happened to these two men?
Though powerful and transformative, these events did
not prove to be the final or culminating experiences of
their lives! They did not solve everything. Marcus
Bach, as a young man, went from his church thinking
he could convert the world, but it did not work out that
way for him. Gopi Krishna experienced something akin

to being out of his mind for 15 years after that meditation. He was deeply disturbed, almost psychotic.

From the whole array of human experiences in mysticism, religion and the psychic, how may we sense the oneness behind these two stories? One approach is to consider all our experiences in terms of the body as an instrument of awareness. We know that the body is capable of a great variety of sensations and feelings. We know also that the body is the temple, where we are to meet God within; it is also a specially constructed instrument for becoming aware of our oneness with God and with all His manifestations in the universe.

The growth of insight from the Old Testament to the New Testament is a movement away from the projection of God "out there" toward an awareness of His existence within the temple of the body. As we think about the symbology of the external temple, or synagogue, or Holy of Holies, it should enrich our understanding of the body as the temple wherein we meet him face to face.

We can think of ritual as a mechanism which awakens our consciousness to processes taking place within us. For example, in the Catholic mass, the transubstantiation brings into view the idea of the presence of Christ. Receiving the symbolic body of Christ into one's body parallels the opening of one's awareness to receive the Christ Consciousness. It is through the system of symbology that wise men of all times and countries have instructed us in the mysteries within.

As the One force flows through us, it may be experienced as rising from within or descending from above. The differences in experiences relate to the different centers of awareness through which the energy flows. Not only in the Edgar Cayce readings, but also in other Western and Eastern sources, we find this concept of the life force flowing through centers which are both senses and rallying points of energy.

In the East these centers, typically seven in number, are referred to as lotuses or *chakras*, the Sanskrit word for wheels, and reside in the spine. The lotuses are depicted as having a specified number of petals each of which is associated with certain symbolic imagery. At the base of the spine, the sleeping serpent kundalini coiled three and one half times, rests asleep. In deep meditation, the serpent awakens and rises through the seven centers to the crown *chakra*, the thousand-petaled lotus. The raising of the energy may be experienced through different channels of the body; however, the yogins working with these experiences and concepts warn us against too quickly associating these experiences with the physical body. The Edgar Cayce readings say the physical, mental and the spiritual bodies are one. With the principle of oneness, we anticipate looking in the flesh body for correlates of mental and spiritual experiences.

As complex, inherent potentials for response, these centers or patterns resemble instincts as we understand them in biology. Carl Jung called these indwelling patterns "archetypes." The Edgar Cayce readings relate these centers and patterns through which the life force flows to the endocrine system. Physiologists know this system to be especially related to motivation, emotion, and feeling, and also, in a very complex, intricate and sensitive way, to the attuned and harmonious functioning of the whole body.

These endocrine glands are seven in number as are the Eastern chakras. The first are the sexual glands, the gonads. The second center is composed of the cells of Leydig located interstitially in the gonads. The third are the adrenals which rest like little golden crowns on the kidneys. The fourth center is the thymus gland placed beside the heart. The fifth center is the thyroid and parathyroid in the neck. The sixth is the pineal located in the brain and higher spacially but not higher in its functioning than the pituitary. Finally, the seventh center is the pituitary, at the top of the spine.

Each gland has a nerve center or plexus (e.g., the adrenals and the solar plexus) and an organ (e.g., the thymus and the heart) associated with it which constitute the centers. The center is not just the endocrine gland alone. The pituitary is associated with a neural complex that is a very special control center in the body called the hypothalamus. Both the pituitary and the hypothalamus are endocrine and neural centers. Working as a team, these constitute the master gland of the body and a kind of throne as the ruling system for the seven centers and the whole body.

Various clairvoyants, sensitives and yogins have depicted these centers in the human body in a variety of ways. According to the interpretation of the Edgar Cayce readings, these centers were correlated with the seven churches in the Revelation of John. (The number seven contains the number three, symbolic of the triune spirit or God, and the number four, symbolic of the elements of the earth. The combination of the three and the four in seven represents the oneness of the heaven and the earth principle within man.) In the Revelation (Rev. 1:4, 4:5) the expression "the seven spirits of God" as seven "churches" or centers within us, gives us a key to understanding patterns of religious, mystical and psychic experiences. If we think of seven as instructive of His nature and not arbitrary symbology, we open ourselves to extraordinary insights regarding the ways in which the One Force may express and be experienced. God manifests in an infinite variety of expressions, but more specifically He manifests through us in seven modes. The One Force may flow through the patterns of the seven major centers in differing combinations and proportions, with differing emphases or inhibitions. Consequently, certain religious practices, such as diet, rituals, music, and expectations, may lead systematically to experiences which are held in common by certain groups.

We are familiar with the Trinity of Father, Son, and Holy Spirit; but we have hardly considered the divine counterpart of the Quaternity, much less its four components and their respective manifestations. The earthly aspects of the Divine are symbolized in the visions of Ezekiel (Old Testament) and John (Revelation) as a calf, a man, a lion, and an eagle. When one or a combination of these four glandular centers is stimulated, the internal process may be given visual or symbolic representation by the figures of these four creatures. On the other hand, as we surround ourselves with depictions of four beasts, the imaginative forces of the mind trigger action of the respective center with which the imagery is associated.

The first of these four lower centers is the gonads, for which red is the symbolic color, earth is the element, and the archetypal vision is the bull, the calf or sacred cow. For primitive man, it was all too clear that his existence depended directly on the germination of seed for crops, the fertility of his cattle, and the propagation of his own children. He was very close to the way the life force perpetuates itself. He came to sense the power of that specific manifestation of the life force and his dependency upon it. He came to pray to that force to appease it, and to develop religious ceremonies and rituals directed to it. We can associate that aspect of the One Force related to reproduction with this first center.

Wherever we find the sacred cow or the bull as an object of worship, we find fertility cults. Here man seeks to relate to the One God with respect to how this force manifests itself in the earth. For example, the first church in the Revelation, the church of Ephesus, was indeed a cult center worshiping Diana as a fertility goddess. We may have difficulty understanding why the Grecians worshipped the multi-breasted Diana or the Hindus the Shiva lingam until we understand that these symbolize one of the ways the life force manifests in the earth plane and through man, which is through the gonad center in this case. The awakening of that center may be stimulated by certain kinds of imagery, certain kinds of rituals, and certain kinds of worship practices. Behind all of this is the One Force manifesting as one of the seven spirits of God.

The second of these archetypal visions of the four beasts is a man. This is of very special symbolic meaning. Man in the earth has a counterpart in the Trinity, in heaven as it were, as the Son or the Christ. The color associated with the endocrine center cells of Leydig is orange and again relates to sexual activity. The hormonal secretion of these cells is testosterone which regulates the expression of masculinity and femininity. This is called the water center, thus symbolic of the Spirit, and correlates to bathing, purification and baptism. Activity of the water center may be symbolized by the fish (which is water materialized), a symbol of the Christ as God *manifest* in the earth, a source of spiritual food. Where you have an outer ritual of baptism, of purification, you have the potential for that same process working within the body. Baptism also symbolizes death of the old life, burial and resurrection to the new life.

This man in the earth of the second center must be raised up to a oneness or a union with the Man in heaven, the Christ as represented by the pineal center. The leyden gland (cells of Leydig) and the pineal are directly connected neurally and constitute a "seat of the soul." This direct connection makes possible a very special experience under optimal circumstances in meditation. The kundalini may be thought to rise up a ladder progressively from center to center. But in the direct relationship of the leyden (an open or closed door) to the pineal (the open door) we have the possibility of the energy rising by the "Appian Way" or the "silver cord" or "the great straight-upward path." Raising this force upward is a resurrection, a return of the prodigal, an alchemical transubstantiation of the elements of the earth into the body of Christ. It is a raising up of the serpent, as in the Old Testament, so that he who looked upon it would not be in danger of being bitten by that force. Thus Jesus said, "If I be lifted up, I will draw all men to me." The raising up of the man in the earth to union with the Man in heaven is the alchemical *mysterium conjunctionis* which is ultimately symbolized in the marriage of the Church, as the Bride, with the Lamb, the Christ, as the Bridegroom.

The third of these lower centers, the adrenals, is symbolized by the lion, or any of the cat family. The spectral color is yellow and the element is fire. There are many religious rituals related to fire, such as the Fijian fire-walking ceremony. When we visited these

Fijians, we were told that they were very religious people, retaining their ancestral practices and being converted Methodists with their own church. Prior to the fire-walking ceremony, the men withdraw themselves for two weeks into a special hut where they refrain from sexual activity, watch their diet and meditate in preparation for walking on a pit of extremely hot rocks with coals of fire around them. What inner motive, when projected outward, seeks to gain mastery over the element of fire?

In this typology, we are associating fire with the lion archetypally. Daniel was not attacked by the lions simply because he was not fearful. Because he was not fearful, his adrenals did not secrete those hormones that would have prepared him to run, flee or fight. Without the secretion of those hormones changing his body chemistry, no vibrations or scents were given off that would mark him as prey. It was, indeed, the protection of God which kept him from attack by the lions, but Daniel's own fearlessness, founded on faith, made available to him the protection against that kind of attack. This principle is very instructive regarding what may happen in religious ritual and in meditation. We gain mastery over all the elements insofar as there is attunement and fearlessness within ourselves. The external rituals which have sought to demonstrate control over the elements have been projections of internal motivations to master the lower emotions.

It is said that the Fijians came by their fire-walking ability when one of their ancestors captured a magical fish which promised to give the man control over fire in return for his release. Symbolically, this was a poor bargain. Frequently when the energy is awakened, symbolized by catching the fish, we sell out for the psychic manifestations of the lower centers, rather than raise it to a pattern of selfless love. The ancient Fijian should have insisted that the fish give him a greater blessing.

The fourth of these lower centers, the thymus, is the heart center, which with the cardiac plexus, and the lungs, is the air center. The heart relates archetypally to love and is symbolized by the eagle, the great birds, or any birds, as these are symbolically expressive of feelings. The highest archetype of the symbology of the birds is the phoenix that dies and is resurrected from its own ashes.

The thymus corresponds to the fourth church in the Revelation which was given love as a virtue and fornication as a fault. These illustrate the range of expression of the emotions related to this center: jealousy, worry, pity, sentimentality. In certain forms of Christianity, this center may be overly stimulated and, when love is awakened out of balance with the virtues of the other churches, may be expressed in fornication. But there is an underestimated power potential of this center as symbolically portrayed in the eagle. The psychic potential of this center relates to overcoming the earth. It may be manifested in psychokinesis or envisioned as UFOs.

In the Revelation, when the energy moves through the open door (the pineal) the four beasts bow down before the throne. They are not destroyed, but they must be obedient.

Psychologically speaking, the activity of the gonads, the cells of Leydig, the adrenals and the thymus must be directed to and integrated by a higher center. Also, psychologically speaking, the motives of worry and love, of anger and hostility, of sexual expression, all must bow down before a higher motivation for the integrated operation of spiritual centers. With the optimum awakening and directing of the kundalini, which happens not instantaneously but over months and years, there is control over the activities of the lower centers by the higher, more spiritual centers. They in turn send forth hormonal messengers symbolized by the Four Horsemen of the Apocalypse to heal and attune the body. The visions of John's Revelation which sound so dire and destructive are actually instrumental in the attunement experience. Once we are on the road and have that spiritual awakening, there is much work to be done to awaken the body to a healing process.

These four beasts may be subsumed under the one

symbol of the dragon which sometimes has the horns of a bull, the head of a man, the tail and claws of a lion, and the wings of an eagle. Carl Jung wrote about the dragon as one of the great archetypes. The dragon imagery in the Revelation relates to the rebellious spirit as it may be expressed through the lower centers.

In moving up to the three higher centers, the thyroid, the pineal and the pituitary, it becomes more difficult to get proper imagery or symbology for those centers because they are not so directly related to the emotions and motivations of the earth dimension. As these centers relate to the Trinity, the thyroid represents the Holy Spirit, the pineal the Son, and the pituitary the Father.

The fifth center is the thyroid, the color is blue or gray, the archetypal pattern relates to the Spirit and the will. The awakening is symbolized in the Bible by the dove and by the Pentecostal tongues of flame.

Religious practices which stress the Holy Spirit experience may deliberately trigger responses from the neck, including the thyroid center, accompanied by speaking in tongues, which some have referred to as "motor (or muscular) hallucinations." There are, to be sure, highly integrative experiences of the Holy Spirit accompanied by tongue-speaking. However, when this center is stimulated out of balance, there may be tongue-speaking which is imbalanced or even pathological.

The sixth center is the pineal, the color is indigo and the symbolic patterns relate to the Light, the open door and the Son or the Christ. Within ourselves, there is a pattern to be whole, not only healthy but also integrated or individuated. Carl Jung referred to this pattern as the archetype of the Self, of which the Christ is the highest symbol. The special role of the pineal center, however, is as the open door. When we have the spirit of obedience as did Jesus, we may say, "Not my will, but thine." The physiological correlate is the release of the pineal, as an open door, to ascendency of the Father, or the pituitary. Jesus' mastery over the lower drives and the wholeness or oneness operative in the higher centers enabled Him to say, "I do what I see the Father doing." We can now more easily understand His saying, "If you have seen me, you have seen the Father."

There has been much confusion in esoteric literature about the pineal as the third eye and its relationship to the pituitary. In some lower animals, the pineal has a physiological function as a "third eye"; however, in man the release of the psychic potential of the pineal to the master gland, the pituitary, constitutes a quantum leap in spiritual evolution. The pituitary, then, becomes the true "third eye." In the temptation in the wilderness, Jesus declined the path of psychic manifestations in favor of the path of obedience. In the garden, he said, "Not my will." This is the spirit of the open door.

Once in a slide presentation on symbology, I had included a photo of an entryway into an Egyptian tomb. I suggested that the entry into the unconscious was sometimes depicted symbolically by movement through a long tunnel with a light at the end. Afterward, a young man came to me and said that the slide had triggered the recall of a dream. In the dream, he was going down a long tunnel toward the light when he came to a 2,000-year-old man. They talked a while and then the man said, "Well, I can see you are not ready for me. Come back when you are ready and we will talk again." Then the man closed the door and the dream ended. I asked the young man, "Who is a 2,000-year-old man?" He said, "Christ! But I'm Jewish!" I replied, "Well, it's your dream and your association!" Apparently he was ready to reconsider the direct implication of the dream as he became very elated in his sharing and reflecting upon it. There is, within each of us, that which may be an open door, when we are ready for Him.

The seventh center is the pituitary, the color is violet, and the fault, from the Revelation, is being lukewarm. As the thousand-petaled lotus, it is also associated with the experience of the white light. It is the "heavenly heart by which life can be regulated" (from *The Secret of the Golden Flower*). As the master gland of the body, it has a complexity and intricacy of action that directs and orchestrates the harmonious functioning of the entire body. It is symbolized by the Ark of the Covenant, the central symbol of the Old Testament tabernacle worship. The Ark contains the "law" which, psychologically, is the "commandment" and the "word" of Deuteronomy 30:11-14, which is written in our mouths and hearts. It is the image of God, in which we were made and to which we, as souls, are destined to conform. (Romans 8:29) It is the mark of the high calling in Christ. (Philippians 3:14) This archetypal pattern of the Self is also related to and should become the *ideal* of each one of us.

Symbolically, the Ark of the Covenant and Noah's ark are the same. Each is a seed which contains a complete pattern of universal law. When opened, these may bring the whole law into perfectly ordered manifestation. The symbolic ark contains within it the symbolic perfect man. Man, as a miniature replica of the universe, contains within himself a pattern of all manifestations. Thus we are like a Noah's ark, with the animals representing all the qualities of motivation and emotion which are indwelling potentials of man.

As we consider the oneness in the concepts of charisma and kundalini, we begin to perceive a oneness in the whole array of religious, mystical and psychic experiences. There is one force and a pattern for attuned or unified functioning within us. In a hierarchy under the pattern of oneness are seven centers, each of which is capable of participating in a unified manifestation or in a harmonious symphony of expression when under the direction of one conductor. Through these seven centers, the seven spirits of God may work, each in its respective pattern. Under each of these seven centers is a descending hierarchy of patterns of expression as symbolized by the people and animals in Noah's ark. Of the people on the ark, there were seven who were obedient and the eighth, Ham, was rebellious. Under these were the animals, seven pairs of all the clean animals and birds and one pair of all the others. (Genesis 7:2-3)

When the energy flowing through these patterns is not directed by a highly motivated singleness of purpose, then an array of motivations and emotions may be expressed in ways which are out of balance, in conflict or at war among themselves. When these variations are given expression in the experiences which are called religious, mystical or psychic, interesting things may happen! The movement of energy may be healthy and in balance (to some the gift of healing, to others the gift of prophecy and so on) or it may be out of balance.

The Edgar Cayce interpretation of the Revelation gives us a key to understanding how that force known as the kundalini (residing at the base of the spine and capable of being raised in meditation) is the same as that force known as the Holy Spirit (which may descend as a dove or a light from above). Both of these are of *one force,* running through different systems. The energy is no different but the circuitry or the patterning through which the energy has flowed has changed. This is the basis for understanding the whole array of experiences from charisma to kundalini; this is the basis of the variations of religious and mystical experiences—the flow of energy through a chosen pattern.

We are always saying, "It's your spirit that counts! You have to have the right spirit! You have to have a selfless spirit!" It is the purpose, the desire and that upon which the mind feeds and dwells that determines the ways in which this energy flows. That desire which opens the whole system to an integrated flow is the motive of selflessness, the motive of love, the desire to be one with the whole. Just as sexual thoughts can awaken one center and thoughts of anger can awaken another, so the highest motivations are those which awaken this system in its most integrated ways.

In the Revelation is a scene in which John sees a book sealed with seven seals. He cries because he knows that no one in heaven or earth is worthy to open those seals. Then comes the Christ who opens them. The instructions to us are that it is only the higher self, the higher motive, the higher spirit within that is worthy to open the seals of the centers. They are not to be opened from a lower desire or motive or manipulation or technique. When the desire is selflessness, we have the optimum opportunity for the awakening of that one energy and its movement through the best circuitry available to man.

The one energy flowing through this system is the source of the highest of the whole array of religious, mystical and psychic experience in both healthy and pathological forms. And the key to the integration of the whole system which puts the highest pattern in control is for the mind to dwell upon the motive of *selfless desire*, the desire to be one with the whole, the desire to be of service.

Working With versus Interpreting Dreams

I began recording my dreams in 1953. I had read about them earlier than that and had been interested in Sigmund Freud's work as early as my high school days. But when I, as a graduate student, told my professors that I would like to do my master's thesis or doctoral work on dreams, they'd say, "Have you read Freud?" I'd say, "Yes," and their jaws would drop as though they were surprised. Then they would say something like, "What is it that you don't understand?" because (in 1958 or thereabout) it was a well-accepted notion, even among psychologists who were not especially interested in Freud, that he had the last word on dreams. His words were these: "There is the dream as you recall it, which is the manifest content, and then there are the associations that you come by only through psychoanalysis which give you the latent content, and only at that point do you have the real meaning." So there was the accepted notion that, unless you had a psychoanalyst working with you, you couldn't really make any progress in your dreams, because the dream you remembered was not important of itself.

Many years later, though, Freud wrote about how difficult it had been for him to get people to work with the manifest content versus latent content idea, and bemoaned the fact that people had gotten so interested in the latent content that they were not looking at the dream itself, a situation he thought unfortunate.

The Freudian approach to analyzing dreams uses free association—which is very difficult, by the way, in the technical sense of Freudian psychoanalysis. You take a portion of the dream, associate to that, then follow up on the associations, and so on, until you have smaller and smaller pieces. What I fear has happened to much of the work that we call dream interpretation is that we start interpreting the dream without looking at the dream itself.

My concern with dreams turned me to the Edgar Cayce readings. I spent two months at the A.R.E. in 1959 and went through as much of the material as was then available; it amounted to about 500 dreams. Now the material covers nearly 1,000 comments by Cayce on dreams and is published in the hardback Library Series in two volumes.

As I began to go through this bulk of material, I applied my Freudian and Jungian knowledge of psycho-analysis to get a feel for what these approaches might have to say about the dream. In almost every case, I was surprised because the readings did not draw the same conclusion as my analyses.

As a matter of fact, and with greater frequency, I found that Cayce's interpretation was shorter than the dream. Now that's noteworthy in and of itself. Most of the time we think of the dream as being compact and the interpretation as a lengthy sequence. All of Cayce's interpretations, however, were concise and exact. He did what Freud said he wished people would do, and that is to see the essential meaning of the dream. Look at the dream and ask yourself what it is saying.

This examination led me to believe that we should work with rather than interpret dreams. For example, I recorded my first big dream in '52 or '53, shortly before my first visit to Virginia Beach. In the dream, I was in a very awkward situation. I was on a platform and an Oriental character was sitting cross-legged behind me. I felt under some kind of spell or under his control. On a scooped-out portion of the platform was a dummy and some water. I was trying to put this dummy under the water to baptize him, and I was saying, "In the name of the Father, in the name of the Son," but I couldn't say, "in the name of the Holy Spirit," because I couldn't get the character under water. With that frustration I mentally experienced a breaking free from the control of the Oriental and a liberation. Suddenly—you know how dream imagery shifts—I was wrestling with a character much taller than myself, who had long grey hair (remember, in 1953 there weren't many people wearing long hair). This was a great hulk of a man, a very muscular, Herculean character, and I'm wrestling with him in a battle to the death. I become aware of a book over to the side. It is written in this book that I will be victorious, so I experience a feeling of assurance. But I know also that not only do I have to wrestle with this one, but that two more just like him are waiting. So I've got three I must wrestle with. I'm exhausted already and I have made little progress. Still I know what is written—I can't understand why they don't know it or why they don't give up, but I have a feeling of confidence.

In interpreting this dream, I'd have to ask myself, "What does the Oriental character mean? What does the baptism mean? What does the control mean? What are the characters?" and so on. But the "working with" approach—and I've worked with this dream for 22 years—is more concerned with wondering about it, reflecting on it. Essentially, the heart of what it means to me is similar to what is the promise in the Revelation, "He who endures to the end will overcome." It identifies for me three major character problems, what I am probably going to have to wrestle with all my life. My identification of those problems is not always the same. Sometimes I rethink that dream and I see that I have something else to work with. But what it gives me is a very special quality about working with the dream and that is to return to the *feeling* of the dream—the emotional content, the awareness, the expanded awareness —and claim and carry that awareness throughout your life. So, at a time when I am feeling low (and all of us are asking the same question in this period from 1958 to 1998) I ask myself: "Am I going to make it this time or not? And, if I don't, I'm really going to blow it because this is a big one, this is important." If I remember this dream at those times, then I become aware of two things: I've been promised that I can make it and must keep on fighting, keep on struggling. It's not just that I have interpreted the dream, but rather it's that I have worked with it as an awareness, a consciousness, an affirmation, an emotional response, something that is uplifting or awakening.

A number of people have come to me with dreams involving Jesus. With some regularity, certainly more than 50%, the person is uneasy about this. He may come to me and say, "I know you're going to think I'm crazy, but I had a dream about talking with Jesus." I find the Cayce readings telling just about everyone who had such a dream that they really had talked with Jesus. But, if you've had such a dream, this ought to result in a special kind of awareness, a promise, something you return to often, something that carries a sense of strong possibility, the potential that it bears for you.

The dream imagery may be used in a mantric way. Now let me differentiate between a *mantra* (which is, say, a syllable like Om and means "mind tool") and the term *mantric*. Rather than saying whether or not something is a mantra, I think a better understanding of it would be to say that we can use something mantricly. Now, in using it mantricly, you awaken a response within the depths of your being. Affirmations should be like this; for example: "Not my will but Thine, O Lord, be done in me and through me." If you can say, "Not my will," really feel it and mean it and respond to it deeply, you get a sense of release. Then you may say you have used that affirmation mantricly. But to repeat a mantra in a rote process and to expect anything to come of it is not to be realistic. As the Master taught us, "Not by rote, but rather by awakening the spirit."

Now, I'd like to stress that in working with the dream, you take the depth of the emotion, awakened by the imagery of the good dream, the big dream, and work with that to reawaken within yourself a sense of the promise, the meaningfulness of life. Remember that it can be a warning just as much as it can be a promise. You may be going about something in a way that you know is not quite right and you're not really comfortable with it. As you know, we all have a way of talking ourselves out of things and into things. For example, you may find yourself with some regularity saying, "I'm not going to do that any more," but through every action you're taking steps and making preparations to go ahead with it. Sometimes our dreams dramatize the outcome of such situations, so that if you reawaken the dream feeling that relates to that circumstance in your life, then you have summoned up an emotional response that's strong enough to help you make the right decision. So, it can work to keep you out of trouble as well as to reawaken a sense of hope and promise about the meaningfulness of life. The dream imagery in this sense has, then, the function of centering, redirecting, reawakening, motivating, reorienting.

A second principle about working with dreams versus interpreting them is simply this basic principle: we are not trying to understand the *dream* but we *are* trying to understand the *dreamer*. It's so tempting, once you have something written down on a piece of paper, to sense that it has an autonomous, independent existence, and you give it to someone and say, "What does that dream mean? What does that symbol mean?" Well, with respect to what?

That's many times a problem with the way we approach our dreams. We don't take the dream *in relation* to anything. As a matter of fact, I think this is the heart of what Edgar Cayce meant when someone asked him about the proper way to interpret a dream. He said, "Correlate those truths." Correlation is a better term perhaps than interpreting—correlating, seeing the relevance of what I have dreamed to what I am doing.

So the meaning of the dream is related to what is going on with the dreamer. Use the dream simply as a way of talking about the dreamer, or a way of looking at yourself. It's not so much that that dream has a meaning, but rather that the dream coming from me gives me some insight about myself. An example: this winter I had a dream in which I was outdoors. There were some bookshelves with books on them and they'd gotten damp and I was dismayed by the fact. Now, a cliche approach to the dream occurs to me—"Left out in the rain." We use an expression "Something's been left out in the rain." So I've got a lot of books that I haven't read, maybe, and maybe I've been negligent in reading and I could say that that portion of my life has been left out in the rain; it hasn't been cared for. But there are some other angles to it, of which you cannot be aware if I merely tell you my dream. For one thing, just the previous night (and I didn't really remember this or make this association until several hours after recording the dream) I remembered that I had driven by this structure late that night and it was just under construction. There was no roof on it, no ceiling to it, and there was a fairly deep emotional response to seeing the rain going into a library sort of building. We had also been moving and I had some boxes of books I had left on a porch. There was a question in my mind about their getting damaged. Now I've got a dream, a cliché answer to the dream, but I've got two personal experiences directly related to that which give me a quite different angle on it. Now I can work with the first interpretation without any of these associations. But once I remember the emotion I felt—and it was similar to what one feels driving along and suddenly working through something daydream-fashion—this response to seeing this building in a dark, foggy, drizzly night, was deeply personal. Looking at that dream and saying, "What does that dream mean?" is really inappropriate. That dream awakened a complex of awarenesses and experiences and concerns within me, that are just not contained in the dream itself in any interpretable way.

So this principle of trying to understand the dreamer, not the dream is central to our process. This may be difficult for you to work with because you have enough experiences so that it seems the dream has a meaning, and you can say, "This dream means this." Then you come to another dream and you say, "Why this is very difficult. I had such good luck with extracting a nice neat meaning from that one. Why can't I do the same with this one?" I think we're in serious trouble if we orient our lives toward a sense of, "I've got to understand that," or "What does this mean?" Someone says, "I was meditating. I had this experience. What does it mean?" It can *mean* many things, but mostly it means something was going on inside *you*.

Victor Frankl, a psychiatrist who at one time held the same chair in medicine that Freud did in Vienna, was also in a Nazi concentration camp. He survived it, but he writes in his book, *Man's Search for Meaning*, that those prisoners didn't survive who had the feeling, "Unless we can get out of here, return to our families, return to our jobs, this will all have been so meaningless." The ones who survived were those who found meaning in what they were doing at the time—making friends with a mouse that was invading their quarters or something similar. Those who responded in a living way to what was going on, he felt, were the ones who truly survived. He is saying that meaning doesn't come from a situation but from your response to it. So, working with a dream as though it were not going to have meaning unless you lay it all out and get a neat interpretation will be misleading for you.

We think of the superconscious and the subconscious, and some people have a notion that the subconscious is underneath and the superconscious is above. However, I find the readings and empirical research rather substantiating the fact that the subconscious rests between our conscious mind and superconscious potential. We are spiritual beings who have the superconscious potential to confront God face to face. What dreaming amounts to is release from the tie to the sensory bodily experience we're caught up in right now. Dreaming is having direct experience. Once freed to experience beyond the conscious tie to the physical senses, we're going to be confronted with one of two things: we're either going to meet God or meet whatever stands between us and our awareness of God.

This applies to the practice of meditation as well. When I turn from the external within, I'm either going to see God, or I'm going to see something I hold in my consciousness in preference to Him. Try it with this simple one minute of silence test. Just measure a minute—a full sixty seconds of silence—and devote that minute to an awareness of the Godhead within yourself. If you don't see it, look at what you spend your sixty seconds on and that will give you an idea of your preference over an awareness of God. Suddenly you may remember an errand and may then ask yourself, "Why do I worry about that, more than wanting to have an awareness of the Divine?"

That's similar to the way dreams work. We have an opportunity for an awareness of the divine within and we will either meet that and experience a superconscious dream, or we see something standing in the way of that. Now, when I say "standing in the way," I mean that as either a stumbling block or a stepping-stone. It depends on how you use it. You can use those things that stand in the way as opportunities to make progress toward an awareness of oneness with Him. So work with your dreams to understand yourself and use those direct dream experiences the way they were meant to be used—as tools for growth and learning.

One dream made a strong impression on me because it was so clear. A young woman, twentyish, on the spiritual path (in her own terms) has a dream of an inviting ocean. She's dashing toward it. There's a wide beach, and there are pieces of glass about a foot tall sticking up on the beach. As she runs toward the ocean she's cutting her feet to shreds. She stops and there's a man there and she's going to complain about why someone had not cleaned up the beach. But as she talks with him, her feet begin to heal. I think she had the first part of the interpretation correct: she senses that the ocean symbolized her spiritual quest and God and the source of all life and she's seeking to return to that, running as fast as she can. But she feels that there are things in the way because of other people's negligence. If you work with the concept of reincarnation and karma, you might get the feeling that she probably put those pieces of glass there herself. But here is one of the great paradoxes of the spiritual quest: we want to charge toward God and we destroy ourselves on those things that we have placed between ourselves and Him; and yet, if we slow down and take time to relate to other people, we can be healed.

I think this would be an excellent dream for her to work with instead of interpreting. Every time she gets impatient with her progress on the path, she should stop and say, "Wait a minute. There's something I've put here on my own path and the more I selfishly try to grow in a spiritual way, *without respect to my circumstances*, the more I'm going to destroy myself. The more I try to cooperate with other people, the more I'm healed."

Another principle in working with dreams is the willingness to work with your whole life. To illustrate this by contrast, there is in certain fields of counseling an approach called "sector analysis," in which the therapist decides to work with just a portion, a segment of the person's life, for example, the financial. He might see that there were personality problems behind the financial problems. He's counseling with respect to a limited aspect of life. Now you can't do this in working with dreams. Dreams *can* be related to the physical, the mental, the spiritual, the financial, the emotional, the problems in your life or the relationships. But you can't make progress in your own growth unless you're also trying to work on whatever parts of your whole life that need attention. You can't just say, "I'm going to work on the spiritual things and forget about the physical." Understand your dreams well, because many times a dream does relate to the physical. If you say, "Oh, I'm not concerned about that," then you're not trying to understand your whole self better. You will not make progress in that area which will inhibit your overall progress.

One of the great ways to make spiritual progress, soul progress, is to write your ideals down on paper. I recommend writing them on the front page of the book that you use for recording your dreams. Rewrite them as you go along. As you are retiring, when you say a prayer for attunement and for receiving that which will be helpful for you, review your ideals, review what you've written down. What is the spirit that you're trying to awaken? How will the attitude that spirit would awaken help you with the problems you're working on? See this process as preparation for good dreaming, guidance dreaming.

Many people ask about programming dreams. That summer in 1959 when I studied the readings on dreams I also was reading the *Tibetan Book of the Dead*. I realized that this is not only a book about how to die, but instructions for the dying person about how to avoid getting caught up in the lower planes of consciousness and how to move on through them. It's not only a book about how to die but also how to dream. Remember sleep is a shadow of the state called death. Very near that time, independently, Leary and Alpert and others had used the *Tibetan Book of the Dead* as a guide for LSD trips. So there is recognition that learning how to die or dream is really knowing how to move in consciousness and not get hung up. For example, it says, "When you get on the other side you'll see two lights: a bright one that will be painful and a dimmer one that is more attractive and will draw you to it because it's more comfortable. Don't go toward the dim light. That's going to be a problem for you. We don't like to face ourselves, you know, in all of that illumination."

So, how to dream or program your dreams? There is no doubt that you can do that. There is excellent empirical or experimental research that shows that you don't even have to work with hypnosis (although it may be effective here). You can work with hypnosis and affect the content of the dream, if you wish. One of the most dramatic experiences in the literature—called the *Petzell Phenomena*—was a study in which slides were presented tachistoscopically (a film shutter exposes the slide for a fraction of a second). It was shown that people who couldn't even claim to have seen the picture remembered the image from the slide in their dreams. For example, one picture of a madonna with a child was shown to a hospital patient who was having considerable anxiety and ambivalence about her relationship with her children. Sure enough, a madonna picture appears in the dream but with some distortion. So whether it is by the slightest suggestion or deep hypnosis, it is shown that you can affect the content of your dreams by pre-sleep suggestion.

I have some misgivings about this—very much like working with the mind to bring things to you that you want without necessarily having a broader spiritual orientation. That it "works" may be deceiving for you. The faith should be in God. The prayer should be for the awakening of the proper ideal. You may go so far as to pray, "Lord, give me that that Thou knowest I have need of." But to say, "I want to have a dream on so and so," seems to be a way of getting a lower consciousness view of that which you're working on. Now obviously this depends on the motivation of the person. I'm talking more about motivation than I am about technique, because someone with a pure and loving heart might use this technique and get good results with it—the good results from the motivation and not from the technique. Try to get a sense of awakening the ideal, awakening the motive, awakening the desire to serve, awakening the desire to be receptive to that which will be helpful to you.

Another aspect of working with dreams is what I would term answer versus solution. Now I find that people, when they pray for a dream about something in their lives, are hoping for one solution. You may pray, "Lord, show me what I can do to become a light to the world..." and then you have a dream which tells you that you need a colonic or something.

You may want to reject the dream as not related to your request, because it didn't seem to contain "the solution." Well, that might have been step one, you see. That's not your solution, but that's *an* answer. It's disappointing when we have some big problem and we're looking for a solution, and many times it's in an unexpected area of our lives. Why do we get answers and not solutions? We first need a sense of direction. This starts with a single step. If we apply it and make a right choice, we're then shown the next step. We get a series of answers that can unfold for us and we grow through the process.

Another related principle is from the work of Carl Jung in which he talks about a deep and profound kind of symbolism in dreaming. Jung sees dreams as presentations of transformation symbolism, growth processes. He says symbols of which you already have a meaningful awareness can't bring you anything new. There's no growth in that. So many times the symbols presented in a series of dreams relates to a growth process taking place over time. Going back to your dream book and looking at symbols in dreams you had a couple of years ago, you see them much more clearly. Well, it's not just that you've got some distance on them, but also you've done some growing. As profound symbolism merges into your life from the unconscious into consciousness, over time it transforms you. You can't suddenly say, "Oh, I know what that symbol means." It's a growth process, a growing into a new awareness. You just can't have the awareness until you've grown through experience, but the dream will precede the complete awareness and help you as you grow. The dream philosophy in the Edgar Cayce readings is sometimes criticized for seeing too much of the good side of life in dreams, and dreams sometimes deal with very "low" emotions. Let me give you a dream to illustrate this and the way in which I see this dream as relating more to the soul than to mundane life. A woman dreams that she has two boyfriends (which she does) and she is visiting the apartments of these two. It's a single building. There is a second-floor and a first-floor. She goes into the lower apartment. It's disgustingly filthy. Everything is in disarray, and she feels very uncomfortable there. Then she goes upstairs to the other boyfriend's apartment and everything is so meticulously clean and orderly that she is uncomfortable there, too. She just feels, "I couldn't live in a place that's like this."

She asks, "I have a feeling the dream is telling me about my considerations of marriage—which one is it telling me I should marry?" Now the question is: does the dream relate to the question as it might relate to the soul in the individual, rather than to her immediate question? I get a different insight. I had the feeling that the dichotomy between these two was more inside of her than it was "out there" and that there was such an ambivalence within her that she had attracted boyfriends who were very different. Her unhappiness with herself was reflected in her discomfort in both their apartments.

We create artificial dichotomies (our society helps us sometimes) we think we have to live by, but neither of them is really us. I felt that this girl needed a more integrated and balanced attitude about life. Until she was willing to confront the grimmer aspects of her life, her spiritual aspirations for perfection would remain uncomfortable beyond her reach and she would likely have an unhappy marriage no matter what happened. Many times the spiritual question takes precedence over the daily life question, and we don't get our daily life straight until we tune in on the inner spiritual problem. "Seek first the kingdom" and the rest will be added. Get the life motivation straight—His will, not our own—and the rest is more likely to follow.

Finally, let me comment on the question of guidance in dreams. I find that many people talk about getting guidance from their dreams, which is all right. I think you can do that. I know people who have worked with that successfully. In my experience, as people relate their guidance dreams to me, I feel that I could see just the opposite interpretation from the one they gave it. In earlier years I would issue a challenge, "You can't give me a guidance dream that tells you to do one thing that I can't interpret to mean another." Well, someone finally challenged me and I had no luck convincing her. She had a dream about bowls and bowls of fruit in this room and she said, "Clearly this dream is telling me to eat more fruit." Well, I wasn't so sure that it was all that clear. It seemed something like excess to me. It could just as easily be saying, "Eat less fruit. You're overdoing it." I find that this happened in response to dreams that were brought to Edgar Cayce. A young woman making extraordinarily careful preparations for motherhood had a dream about eating chocolate and Edgar Cayce said, "Then eat more chocolate," and she didn't understand. She responded, "Well, I haven't been eating chocolate. I don't know why I had this dream," and she wasn't prepared to get information counter to her preconceived notions about what would make a proper diet for her. She once said, "Chocolate is bad," so she couldn't work with a dream that seemed to recommend it for her. So let's be very careful about "guidance" dreams.

The Edgar Cayce readings outline a procedure for validating our interpretations of dreams. First, pose the question about your dream so that it can be answered yes or no. Then from the reasoning, rational mind answer it yes or no. After you make a decision, meditate for attunement. Do not *meditate on the question*. This is an attunement period. Following that, ask the question deep within yourself, "I have decided 'yes' on this. Now, is it yes or no?" Edgar Cayce says this is a way His Spirit bears witness with our spirit. It's a very challenging approach to decision-making. So let me say at least this—that if you are talking about guidance dreams, check them out through this approach. (If you're not familiar with this approach you may want to read about it. It's in the A.R.E. Circulating File on *Meditation;* also the file on *Will: Decisions* describes this procedure in more detail.)

Of course there's a great deal of literature on dream interpretation. I encourage you to study and work with your dream experiences but do avoid analyzing dreams and get a broader sense of what this is all about. We are spiritual beings who have the potential for an awareness of our oneness with God. The dream has the potential to help us grow in that awareness, and it's a very complicated thing with every aspect of our life. In turning to the dream, because it's a step toward a closer awareness of Him, we get a different angle on what's happening, a different approach to ourselves. It will always be worth your while to work with this material, even if you don't sense that you're getting the right interpretation. One works with the dream, considering the way to grow with it over time. Please don't get discouraged or disappointed because you can't seem to interpret a particular dream; just "be" with it and watch what develops.

Psychosomatic Health

Psychosomatic, by definition, means "a branch of medical science dealing with interrelationships between the mind or emotions and the body" and ". . . bodily symptoms or bodily and mental symptoms as a result of mental conflict." Psychosomatic illness is the manifestation of the detrimental effects of mental processes on the physical body. Psychosomatic health then would be the beneficial effects of the mental processes on the body. If there can be psychosomatic illness, then there can surely be psychosomatic health.

The supreme and ultimate manifestation of psychosomatic health is seen in the resurrection of Jesus who overcame even the death of his physical body. The resurrection of the body, according to the Edgar Cayce readings, is a potential for all of us in our spiritual evolution. Our destiny as souls is with the Father Who created us. The destiny of the body is our own responsibility. Will we take back to the Father the gift of a resurrected body? This concept is delineated in the readings in *A Search for God*, Book II, in which the destiny of the mind, the destiny of the body and the destiny of the soul are addressed. Death is, to be sure, the last to be overcome by us all as is stated in the Scriptures. Nevertheless, this promise of overcoming death is a very special opportunity for us and there are invaluable instructions on this in the readings.

The readings state there are, to this day, some living in the earth plane who have not yet experienced physical death. A young man who came to Edgar Cayce received several hundred readings. He was told that he could regenerate his body and could live indefinitely if he followed the information given and stayed on the track which he was following at the time. Such a promise is incredible for most of us; but if we keep in mind the whole story of how we got involved in the earth and how we are to get free of the earth, we might consider the possibility more seriously.

In order to understand our present state, we can work with a triune formula—and this is the key to psychosomatic health: 1) the Spirit is the life; 2) the mind is the builder; and 3) the physical is the result. The Spirit is the One Force, the source of all life and therefore of all healing and transformation. What the mind as the builder does with that one energy is manifested in our physical reality. Thus, the physical is the result of the spirit as challenged by the mind.

Most of the time when we think of healing, we think of physical healing; however, we must keep in mind that physical illness of itself is merely a symptom. The body is a symptomatic manifestation of what we have done with our access to the Divine energy, the One Force. In some incarnation, we must take this mind and will of ours, grab them by the scruff of the neck and bring them into alignment and attunement with the One Law, the One Force. If we are not able to achieve this control now, we will have another chance . . . *but* the opportunities may not be as great, life may not be as comfortable, and the challenge may be much more demanding for us. Therefore, no matter what our present age or condition of our health, we should set about doing what we know to be right. There will then be a healing effect on the physical, but more importantly on the mental and spiritual bodies.

The term "psychosomatic" was coined in the 1920s. With the psychoanalytic approach to the analysis and symbology of dreams, there developed an awareness of the symbolic psychodynamics of physical illness. The first statements of psychosomatic relationships were rather naive and over simplified and did not begin to do justice to the complexity of the relationship between the body and the mind. A complete understanding of psychosomatics requires not only full understanding that mind is the builder but also accepting the concept of reincarnation.

According to the earlier theories, a person might have hay fever or sinus trouble because inside he was crying, or he might have a sore neck because he was stiff necked in attitude. Such analysis of psychosomatic relationships seems occasionally to be accurate. However, the full scale of these relationships is far, far more complex. There is a more intricate lawfulness to these interactions which in time will be discovered.

In the meantime, most of us have grown up feeling that the body works chemically and automatically with no interrelationship with our emotions. We know if we get angry, we feel it in our stomach, but we do not think that getting angry has anything to do with improper digestion of a meal. We separate the psychological functioning from the health of the body. Psychosomatic medicine says tension caused by stress or strain will have an effect on the body. Although we have come to accept this in a sense, we tend not to apply it to ourselves in our daily lives.

Behind this relationship between the mind as the builder and the physical as the result is this controversial idea: all illness comes from sin, be it of body, of mind, or of the soul manifested in the earth. To define "sin" we may say it is essentially noncompliance with universal law, ignorance of the way things work. The full implication of this definition extends to errors in previous life behavior and patterns manifesting in the present incarnation.

The relationship of sin to illness is made clear in the teachings of Jesus. He saw a paralytic to whom He said, "Take up your bed and walk." Those about Him complained about this but He replied, "Thy sins are forgiven." They said, "Who is this that blasphemes that He can say He forgives sins?" Jesus asked, "Which is easier to say, 'thy sins are forgiven' or to say, 'take up your bed and walk?'" More than just a kernel of truth is contained in this intimation of a relationship between physical disorder and the thought or behavior disorder that we would call sin.

Individually, we are a law unto ourselves. This is well documented in a book entitled *You Are Extraordinary* by biochemist Roger Williams. He has demonstrated that some people, to get the same effect, may need as much as 200 times more of a particular vitamin than others. We are biochemically unique, our needs are unique and that to which our bodies respond is unique. To know what is lawful for us, we must learn the general rules as well as discover specific rules which apply uniquely to our own bodies. We should rejoice and take special note when we make these discoveries.

There are laws that can be discovered and followed for the benefit of our bodies. For example, a young man was looking forward to his 18th birthday so he could begin drinking. He and several friends began to frequent different spots where they could drink beer. Within a few weeks, he developed a serious case of sinusitis. When he did not drink any beer for a couple of days, his nasal congestion cleared. As soon as he began drinking again, his sinusitis reappeared. It dawned on him that he was allergic to beer. He had the good sense to give it up. Beer did not agree with his system and persisting in drinking it was not worth the discomfort. Had he persisted in the behavior, the nasal congestion could properly have been said to be a consequence of sin.

There are also laws regarding the expression of emotions and attitudes, such as resentment or anger. Negative feelings trigger specific psychological responses which may harmfully manifest in the physical body. These are laws and we cannot escape from their functioning within our physical selves. As an illustration of the lawful step-by-step complexity of the development of a psychosomatic illness, let us examine in full detail reading 1749-1.

Mrs. Cayce: You will go over this body carefully, examine it thoroughly, and tell me the conditions you find at the present time; giving the cause of the existing conditions, also suggestions for help and relief of this body. You will answer the questions she has submitted as I ask them:

Mr. Cayce: Yes, we have the body, [1749].

Now, as we find, there is rather the complication of disturbances in the physical forces of the body. These arise from several causes or disturbances.

In the first we find there has been the inclination for the body, through activities of the mental self in its anxiety, to raise or open the centers of the body through meditation and activity when the physical forces were not in the condition for such.

Notice first the primary cause of the problem: she was trying to have a meditation experience, to open the spiritual centers, when she was anxious and when her physical body was not prepared for such an experience.

This produced upon the nerve system, especially the sympathetic, what might be called a contaminated stream of negative reaction; causing or producing a nervous breakdown.

The "contaminated stream of negative reaction" probably refers to secretions from the adrenals associated with anxiety.

Then this slowed the activity of the *physical* body-action in relationships to the mental and spiritual self; in much the same manner as would be the short-circuiting of the nervous system to the high vibratory forces of bodily functioning.

This is the key to the subsequent problems: the lack of coordination between the physical, mental and spiritual. In the body, this is a lack of coordination in the various functions of the nervous system.

Hence we have those effects as seen in the auditory forces being under suppression—or in the eustachian tubes the inclination for this slowing to produce a catarrhal condition.

This caused or produced a prolapsus, or dropping down. Hence we have had buzzing, and gradually the hard of hearing—or the ear filling; causing the inner ear to become static as it were in its activity.

Again we find the digestive system upset by the same character of slowing of activity of the secretions from the lacteals, or the balancing between the acidity and alkalinity for the necessary digestive forces.

This produced then a state of unbalanced fermentation in the stomach. Then this caused more nervousness, more of physical gas and a pressure which produced a disturbing condition.

This caused headaches and dullness, and with the natural condition as broken between the sympathetic and cerebrospinal nervous system a lulling of the activity of the system towards digestion and elimination. Accumulations of poisons are a natural result of such disturbing conditions. This makes for a lethargic reaction then to kidneys, as well as liver and spleen and pancreas—and the effect of the reaction of an anemic condition, or the lack of the coordination between the deeper and the superficial circulation.

All of these have been and are a part of the disturbance to this body.

The effects at various times are suppression to the lungs or pulmonary system; at others the overactivity of the kidneys, at others the tendency for the whole general system to produce that of melancholia—the inclination for the body to become so overexercised as for the lachrymal ducts to overflow, or for the inclination to cry, to weep, and to feel sorry for self.

All of this produces greater depressions through the system.

As we find, in making applications for the body that would correct the disturbance:

Notice the first step recommended now for psychosomatic health: developing a sense of personal contact with the Master.

First, quiet the self mentally, internally, by holding to those things which are eternal—such as may be found in reading the 14th, 15th, 16th and 17th of John.

This sermon of Jesus begins with, "Let not your heart be troubled: you believe in God, believe also in me." (John 14:1) This is the most helpful and important assurance we may receive from the Bible. An A.R.E. publication, *A Closer Walk,* deals specifically with the text of John 14–17 and readings relating to it. This book is so important that it should be carried with us, put under our pillow while sleeping, and memorized, verse by verse. The readings urge us to read a few verses at a time and apply them each day. Now the reading elaborates on the importance of these verses:

Know that these words, in the reading of same though the names of others may be used, do not apply other than to thy inner self. Do not read these merely as rote, but as experiences to thine own inner self.

As ye read, "In my Father's house," know that it means in *thy* Father's house, in thy own soul, in thy own experience are the many mansions! And "were it not so, I would have told you," means that if it were not so ye yourself would have known; ye yourself may experience same through His presence and His abiding faith in *thee,* as well as that thou may have in Him!

Then, through such corrective measures as might be administered by Dr. Miller, have—gently but firmly—a relaxing first of the lumbar centers, gradually going upward to the rest. For in these areas were the centers first opened. Such would be done firmly, making adjustments and a gentle massage through the centers in the lumbar, the lower dorsal, then gradually to the upper dorsal and through the cervical areas.

Osteopathic adjustments are recommended by the readings as the basis for all physical healing.

Following such relaxings, have the gentle, soothing, low electrical vibrations as may gently heat the body throughout. Not the sinusoidal, not the deep therapy, but the general static, that may be applied for twenty to thirty minutes, with the body remaining quiet.

Afterward hold thy deep meditation as you rest, and let this be that ye would follow within thyself, and with thine own words:

"Father, God! Thy handmaiden comes before thee seeking grace, mercy, truth, understanding!

"Open my heart, my mind, to Thy love. And use Thou me, O Father; not as I would but as Thou seest that I may serve Thee better; that I may be the more perfect channel for the manifesting of Thy love to the children of men."

We are through for the present. 1749-1

What does Cayce recommend for this extraordinarily complicated disease process? Very simply: 1) work in a living way with the Bible; 2) get a series of osteopathic adjustments and electrical treatments; and 3) read and meditate with a real sense of the presence of the Spirit working within.

We spoke earlier of the complexity of the psychosomatic relationship. To illustrate this, the following list contains the steps involved in the development of the disorders given in the reading we have just studied:

Anxiety and the body not being in condition to cope with it led to opening of centers in meditation, which led to a contaminated stream of negative reaction resulting in a nervous breakdown.

With the slowed coordination among the physical, mental and spiritual, there was auditory suppression, eustachian tubes slowing, a catarrhal condition and a prolapsus; this led to buzzing, becoming hard of hearing, and inner ear static.

With the digestive system upset, there came imbalanced acidity-alkalinity and improper digestive forces.

These led to unbalanced fermentation in stomach, more nervousness, gas, pressure, headaches, dullness, lulling of the digestion and elimination.

These were followed by accumulation of poisons, lethargic reaction to kidneys, liver, spleen and pancreas.

These were followed by anemia, incoordination of the deep and superficial circulation, suppression of lungs and pulmonary system, and overactivity of the kidneys.

The final outcome was melancholia accompanied by extensive crying.

The following reading, 69-4, is another case which is very instructive for a fuller understanding of psychosomatic relationships:

Mrs. Cayce: You will have before you the body and enquiring mind of [69] present in this room, who seeks information, advice and guidance, as to how she may be a perfect channel, physically, mentally and spiritually, for fulfilling the purpose for which she entered this experience. You will answer the questions, as I ask them:

Mr. Cayce: Yes, we have the body, the enquiring mind, [69], this we have had before.

In giving advice or counsel, regarding making the body a channel for manifestations of *His* purposes with thee—as is understood by the entity, there is that within self which when attuned to the divine is filled with the renewal of life forces, life influences and purposes. Yet there is the continual warring of flesh, or materiality, with the spiritual influences.

As we have indicated heretofore, and as we find existent in the present, there are physical disturbances of such natures as to hinder or to prevent that full realization of the abiding presence of the Christ Consciousness. Yet there is the realization that it *is*, that it exists, that it helps, and that it is the *only* source of healing for a physical or a mental body.

Let us stress this point: ". . . The Christ Consciousness . . . is the *only* source of healing for a mental or physical body."

Yet how may there be that attuning to that divinity, that promise?

By emptying self of all that so easily besets, and *doing*, being that as fully known, fully comprehended by the entity.

Then know—as those of old, through their experience of material disturbance, mental unrest—if thou art willing, He will direct. Then let Him have His way with thee.

For, as is understood, He hath not willed that any soul should perish; yet because there are disturbances of a physical, material or mental nature, one oft doubts, and fears arise. These beget those influences that prevent the proper attunement.

The readings indicate that doubt, then fear, is a major cause of many illnesses and the problem of fear seems to be universal. We are encouraged, as we place our faith in Him, to doubt not!

To be sure, such oft appears at variance to that comprehended or experienced by others, or visioned in the experience of others. Yet know that by thine own individuality, thine own purpose, He is mindful of thee; and as ye find—thyself—that way He hath conceived as the better for the fulfilling of the purpose for which ye entered this experience. For, ye *would* be one with Him.

Then, let that mind be in thee as was in Him. Those who rebuked Him for the needs of suffering, He rebuked in no uncertain manner.

Now, regarding having the mind of Christ, study carefully Philippians 2:5-8. "Those who rebuked Jesus" may refer to Jesus' statement "get thee behind me, Satan" when Peter questioned the necessity of His having to die. "Those who rebuked Him for the needs of suffering, He rebuked in no uncertain manner."

Thus each entity, each individual, must realize this through his own attunement. Ye must *know* that He walks with thee. And, as has been indicated, there should come that experience of thy *hearing* His voice. When in attune ye will, ye do. For, as He has given, "I stand at the door and knock; if ye will open, I will enter."

This is to be, this *is* then an individual experience—for each soul that seeks His presence.

Think not that He has not heard, because it has not yet appeared so, or because thou hast not yet heard Him save in the lives and the experiences of those thou hast helped.

Seek not then thy way of manifestations, but more and more, "Here am I, Lord; use me, send me. Point the way that Thou would have me go."

This is a promise to thee, to each soul; yet each soul must of itself *find* the answer within self. For indeed the body is the temple of the living God. There He has promised to meet thee; there He does. And as thy body, thy mind, thy soul is attuned to that divine as answers within, so may ye indeed be quickened to know His purpose; and ye may fill that purpose for which ye entered this experience.

It is not then by justifying but in *glorifying* the good, the true, the beautiful, that thou hast seen in Him.

Belittle not those things that hinder. These are a part of thy cross, of that necessary; else He, according to His promise, would not allow these to be a part of thy awareness.

For, know—as He hath given—"Lo, I am with thee always, even unto the end." This is not a mere saying, but an awareness which one may find through that attuning through meditation, through prayer, through opening of self for direction by Him.

Ready for questions.

Q-1. Regarding the physical: Please advise as to diet.

A-1. . . . We would add those foods that tend to make the eliminations improved; that is, fruits—fresh or raw; as well as cooked; and we would include those that produce better eliminations—figs, raisins, grapes, pears, and the like.

. . . To be sure, it may be asked here, *why* does the system keep producing refuse or poison—when the body attunes self, and the body desires health, and the body keeps in accord with that which is of a spiritual import?

Would this woman continue to have problems even if she were doing everything she knows to do? We must not expect complete instantaneous results. The continuity of life and patterns from previous incarnations must be considered.

This is a result of disobedience of *laws*—not only in the present; for *life* is the whole, not an individual experience!

For, impulses arise, and tendencies; and ye would be every *whit* whole!

Remember, as He gave, "The heavens and the earth will pass away—my word shall *not* pass away; but ye shall give *account* for every *deed* done in the body!"

Hence we find *law*. Law is love, yes—as love is law; yet God is not mocked, whatsoever ye sow, that must ye reap.

If ye reap it in *Him*, He bears the cross with you.

In the purifying of the system, remember it is the active principle of these influences indicated that works *with* the divine within—as with that law—to produce *attunement* to a normal balance *in* an individual entity. Thus, what is at times to some upsetting is to another creating a balance . . .

Q-7. *Regarding the Mental and Spiritual: Is there any specific work I should be stressing in my activity at this time?*

A-7. This had best come from that as the body-entity receives in its *own* meditation, rather than being directed by any outside influence. For, it is the willingness, the desire, the try that is counted in the righteousness of each entity, each soul. And these directions are from Him, as direction is sought.

Q-8. *How may I overcome the innate doubt or fear which prevents attunement with the Christ, as promised?*

A-8. Just keeping on keeping on in the trust—trust—

in Him! No *direct* way may be experienced for self by another—and yet the entity finds self very oft close to being directed in that way. Hold fast to Him!

Let that which causes doubt or fear be taken up in the willingness, the desire, to be of help to others.   69-4

Notice specifically the stress on the willingness to have doubt and fear replaced by the desire to be of help to others. Even though she has been given the assurance of being aware of His presence, she is anxious about this not being so. There is yet doubt and fear in the face of such a promise!

Notice also the reference to reincarnation. Just because we begin putting everything right in our life does not mean we do not have anything else to meet. Also notice the attitude that is suggested: "Belittle not those things that hinder, these are part of your cross, of that necessary; else He, according to His promise, would not allow these to be part of thy awareness...which one may find through that attuning through meditation, through prayer, through the opening of self for direction by Him."

Now let us sample a few of the thousands of readings which deal with psychosomatic illness. There may be a combination of causes both in mental attitudes and physical neglect:

Q-1. What is the physical explanation of hives, and how may I overcome this condition?

A-1. These are from lack of proper eliminations and of allowing self to become aggravated and breaking the connections between cerebrospinal and sympathetic nervous systems. For this usually, as we find, comes from the area of the diaphragm and this is rather a combination. But with the character of treatments indicated the general attitude being more constructive and less of animosities, less of holding grudges or those things which make the entity speak of others unkindly, these will be overcome, for these destructive attitudes bring on self all the pent up feelings and they find expression in irritations.   5226-1

Anger is especially a destroyer of health, as well as of relationships:

... For anger can destroy the brain as well as any disease. For it is itself a disease of the mind.   3510-1

Do not *belittle*, do not *hate*. For hate *creates*, as does love—and brings turmoils and strifes. [Author's italics]   1537-1

And here we find that *hate* and *animosity* and anxiety may be the poison that causes *much* of the disturbance. [Author's italics]   1196-11

The attitudes, then, should be such that there is *no* animosity, *no* feelings of resentments—but a forgiving, loving expression towards *all* about the body—in *every* form and manner.   1196-12

There are many today who are advocating the open expression of negative feelings and emotions. There seems to be no support for such therapies from the perspective of the readings.

... The entity gave way to the material things, and self-indulgences brought in the latter portion of that period regrets—that, next to *jealousy*, sap the *spiritual purpose* in the mental attributes of body and mind of an individual manifested in materiality.

Thus the lesson to the entity: Do not let regret, jealousy, become a part of thy mental experience. These ye can control in thy mental self. Not always easy, but putting that purpose forth as indicated—the hope, the desire, the faith in the promise of Him—He may take away thy burdens. [Author's italics]   2390-7

Then, as we have indicated, *know* in *whom* as well as in *what* ye believe. *Know* that the influence of Good, or God, is able—then—to bring about those influences that will fit the body—physically, mentally, spiritually—to fulfill that purpose—that is, in body, mind and

**soul—for a better, a greater, a broader service in the
spiritual direction.**   **1196-10**

Always there was given encouragement. It is never
too late, no matter how far astray we may have gone.

There is no question of the reality of psychosomatic
illness. More importantly, in fact imperatively, we must
claim and put into action the positive side of this
process: psychosomatic health. The Edgar Cayce readings give the strongest imaginable encouragement to us
to expect healing of every kind.

Consider the following statements of encouragement, instruction and assurance. Read and reread them
and allow them to quicken expectancy and determina-
tion to seek and manifest healing of every kind in your
own life:

At *times* we find these conditions get on the nerves
of the body, as it were, and the body ceases to care to
put up the resistance, feeling as if there is no use. This
should be dismissed, for the body should acquire and
gain, and set before self, that *all building and replenishing
for a physical body is from within, and must be
constructed by the mind of the entity*; for *Mind is the
Builder*; for each cell in the atomic force of the body is
as a world of its own, and each one—each cell—being
in perfect unison, may build to that necessary to
reconstruct the forces of the body in all its needs...
[Author's italics]   93-1

Remember, the body does gradually renew itself
constantly. Do not look upon the conditions which have
existed as not being able to be eradicated from the
system.

The person asked for other helpful suggestions and
was told:

Hold to that KNOWLEDGE—and don't think of it
as just theory—that the body CAN, the body DOES
renew itself!

**Then keep those portions of the body active that
do this; and we will find these conditions will—in a
little while—be a thing of the past.** [Author's italics]
1548-3

One person asked, "Have my present physical
difficulties any connection with an accident that occurred many years ago?" and was told:

**Only in so much as the mind allows self to associ-
ate same with the accident. For, as we have indicated,
*the body renews itself according to the mental attitude
it holds toward ideals, and in the light of the application of relationships to others.* And this applies as well
in the relationships to self.** [Author's italics]   **2081-2**

**. . . No condition of a physical nature should be
remaining unless it has been hamstrung by operative
forces or strictures or tissue that may not be absorbed;
and even this may be changed *if it is taken patiently
and persistently—in any body!*** [Author's italics] **133-4**

"Is it possible for our bodies to be rejuvenated in
this incarnation?" someone asked. The readings responded:

***Possible.* For, as the body is an atomic structure,
the units of energy around which there are the move-
ments of the atomic forces that—as given—*are ever
the sentiment or pattern of a universe, as these atoms,
as these structural forces are made to conform or to
rely upon or to be one with the spiritual import, the
spiritual activity, they revivify, they make for constructive forces.***

**How is the way shown by the *Master?* What is the
promise in Him? The last to be overcome is death.
Death of what?**

**The *soul* cannot die; for it is of God. *The body
may be revivified, rejuvenated.* And it is to that end it
may, the body, *transcend* the earth and its influence.**

But not those standing here may reach it yet!
[Author's italics]   262-85

This final statement from the readings is especially
applicable and we may begin a consciousness of good
health by working with these principles and meditating
with this affirmation for healing. Someone asked, "How
can I best prepare for old age?" The reading said:

By preparing for the present. Let age only ripen
thee. For one is ever just as young as the heart and the
purpose. *Keep sweet. Keep friendly. Keep loving, if ye*
would keep young. [Author's italics]   3420-1

Q-4. Is there a meditation that can be used for
building the body and keeping it in good condition? ...
A-4. Just as the suggestions may be used that have
been made to the body through some of the treatments
outlined—the *mind* acts upon the resuscitating forces
of the physical being, by and through suggestion. Just
so there may be the realization that spiritual forces are
a part of the whole physical being. For, the *real* being
is the spiritual import, intent and purpose, see? Thus a
meditation, a centralizing, a localizing of the mind
upon those portions of the system affected, or upon the
activities needed for the physical being, *influences*,
directs the principal forces of the system. And it does
resuscitate, if kept in sincerity; not merely said as rote,
but that said being put into practical application through
the experiences and associations with others—and especially this entity as it works with the developing
minds, may see such reactions.

In the meditations, then, *open* the mind, the
being, to the influences about same; surrounding self
with the consciousness of the healing that is in the
Christ Consciousness, the Christ-awareness.

Thus:
Lord, use Thou me—my body, my mind—in such a
way and manner that I, as Thy servant, may fill those
lives and hearts and minds I meet—day by day—with
such hope and faith and power in Thy might, that it

may bring the awareness of Thy presence into the experience of others as well as myself.

Such as these will bring those forces and influences for helpful experiences for the body.   1992-3

Use of the Life Force as Sexual, Psychic or Spiritual Energy

Man is a user of energy. Not only does he use energy but he emanates energy. Not unrelated to the spiritual problem of our time is one of today's most serious challenges called "the energy problem." As a user of energy, man deals with all kinds of power: atomic, nuclear, hydro-electric, petroleum, solar, and so on. We are actually internal combustion engines: we take in calories, burn them and expend them in physical activity. Beyond that is another kind of internal energy within our being. The question of the quality and nature of this energy has led to the development of an entire field of study called dynamic psychology.

Sigmund Freud was concerned with locating the energy involved in manifestations of creativity, religious experience and in relationships with one's fellow man. He was looking for misdirections of this energy in his study of psychopathology.

A scientist colleague of mine who has written 50 books told me, "In science always keep your eye on the energy!" This question of energy is an extremely serious one in many fields of study. The field of parapsychology, for example, has only recently begun its proper inquiry into "keeping an eye on the energy." In laboratories, researchers had previously looked at the phenomenon of ESP in relation to the significance of scores, the hits or misses. Now many parapsychologists are beginning to look more carefully at the energy as it manifests in psychokinesis, psychotronic generators, healing and Kirlian photography.

If we work with the basic premise from the Edgar Cayce readings that all force is One, then we have some reconciling to do with what seems to be an array of different kinds of energies. Externally, it is not clear to us how eletrical energy relates to gravity or how gravity relates to magnetism. Physicists are now saying there are four kinds of forces: two inside the atom and two outside—one strong and one weak, in each case. However, Einstein worked with "the law of one" in looking for a unified field theory. He wanted to see, for example, how gravitational force might relate to the electromagnetic forms of it. If Einstein could have studied the Cayce readings, he would have gained insights that would have been extremely helpful and illuminating to him in his quest.

According to Cayce, man is a gatherer, transformer, transducer and a worker with the one force. The total human body consists not only of a physical body but mental and spiritual bodies as well. Among these "bodies" there are points of contact relating us to the universe as unique individuals. These points of contact may be referred to as chakras or spiritual centers and correspond to the endocrine system.

Within ourselves we have an inner energy which flows in a manner analogous to the polarity of an electrical system. This electrical system may be likened to a battery with the cosmic force as its energy source. We see electrical energy as either positive or negative, but actually there is only one force. (This philosophy is called bipolar monism.) We have within us something like the poles of a battery. Let's pursue this analogy further. If we laid a wrench across the poles of an automobile battery, what would happen? The wrench would melt because of the extraordinary amount of energy flow. On the other hand, if we connect two leads from an FM radio to the same battery, we may tune in on a rock station, a soul station, a station playing music of the '30s and '40s, or a classical music station. The varieties in those stations are all matters of vibration and attunement, but the same energy is the source of these different qualities of vibration or music. We, too, pick up emanations of vibration waves from some distant power source, which is analogous to telepathy or spiritual attunement.

In pursuing this problem, let us consider the difference between two widely divergent, seemingly unrelated kinds of experience: kundalini and charisma. A man like Gopi Krishna sits quietly in meditation and feels the force rising within; and a man like Marcus Bach, who was working with the Pentecostal movement, prays and then feels a light and a force descending from without. If we work with the principle of the oneness of all force, then a oneness must be seen between this serpent, kundalini, and this dove, the Holy Spirit. Yes, this does dramatize a seemingly unlikely union, but the principle of the oneness of all force requires us to consider how these energies might be one and the same force.

Now, what is the difference? The difference is in the circuitry through which the energy flows. We may think of the centers within us, those points of contact, as different kinds of circuitry through which the one force may flow.

In terms of our use of the life force, sexual, psychic and spiritual energy are all the same energy, just *one* energy. The way in which it is given manifestation depends on the selection of the circuitry, or station of attunement, through which it flows. What selects the circuitry? If we understand that, we will have a physiology, and not just a psychology, of sublimation.

Sexual Energy

The Cayce readings suggest that there is not a soul incarnate in the earth plane today but for whom dealing with this aspect of energy is not a major problem. It has been my impression, through talking with hundreds of people attempting to move into the spiritual life or work in a spiritual way, that one of the most resisted insights is the full implication of the relationship between sexual energy and spiritual energy.

A few years ago, we visited several new age communities in New Mexico. One of these was organized by a well-known yogi, who had several ashrams around the country which he visited periodically. On one of his visits to this particular commune, someone made the mistake of asking him if sex were allowed. His answer was "No!" Shortly afterward when we visited them, these young people were very distraught. They had come to a crisis situation in their lives: sex had been a part of the activity of the commune and the yogi's answer was much to their dislike. They were at a point of critical choice on the spiritual path. They wished they had not asked.

The Cayce readings say that in every age when there is a growth toward a deep spiritual awakening of universal love, it is accompanied by the problem of free love. With the awakening of greater powers, with the awakening of higher energies, with the consciousness of universal law, the brotherhood of man, with the reawakening of past-life memories and discovering people with whom we have worked and loved, there is the opening up of memory and energy. This is a very special kind of thing to meet. It is beautiful! It is challenging! And it is potentially one of the most difficult things with which we have to deal.

We need to put at rest one myth that surrounds the physical expression of sex—that there is a requirement or physical imperative for sex. A few years ago, we met a young man about 26 years of age, who said he had been a heroin addict for 20 years. His addiction, according to him, was psychological and not physiological. "It is all in the mind," he stressed. "You can have a man in prison for 20 years who hasn't touched heroin during that period of time, but there's something going on in his mind about what he's going to do when he gets back on the street. It's all in the mind."

Therefore, although the Cayce readings indicate that there are biological urges to be met, it is clear that the problem does not lie in biology but in what the mind builds for the self. We now have the basis for a profound understanding of what selects the circuitry. It is the mind—not the intellect—but the mind in a broader sense.

We can demonstrate this concept to ourselves with electronic measuring equipment such as that used in psychophysiological laboratories. When we talk about physiology, we are talking about electricity and biochemistry. For a demonstration experiment, the subject is attached to electronic equipment to monitor brain waves, heart and respiration rate, and galvanic skin reflex. He is asked to think of a number from 1 to 5, not reveal it to anyone, and answer "no" to each question. He has chosen "3." "Is it number 1?" "No." "Is it number 2?" "No." "Is it number 3?" He replies, "No," but the needle instantaneously blips. There is a change in the biochemistry of the body when a person responds untruthfully. A single word (like the number 3), previously a neutral word which the individual has simply selected for the moment, now triggers marked physiological responses. When we explore the biochemistry associated with that response, we look to the endocrine system and the autonomic nervous system. What has selected the circuitry for response to this experience? The mind. With the mind we can, like a push-button radio, select any of the circuitries of love, anger, sex or worry as the channel through which energy will flow.

Sigmund Freud has received much criticism for building a whole theory of psychology around sexual energy. His libido theory specified strongly that his energy was the basis of all creativity, religious experience and psychopathology. When we look at the Cayce readings or kundalini yoga, we find the same teachings: that one of the poles of our inner battery is the center related to sex, the gonads. Cayce called the sexual system the motor or the generator. The Cayce readings are delightful in their gentleness, firmness, insight, acceptance and encouragement about working constructively with this energy. Kundalini yogans teach about a root chakra at the base of the spine from which the kundalini rises. When raised, this powerful force can transform sexual energy into psychic or spiritual energy.

A 50-year-old woman was given an extraordinary reading. She was told that if she were to pass through a throng of men without speaking, all of them would follow if they were free to do so. Yet, if this attractiveness were properly used, it would bring help to many individuals. She became very disturbed because, apparently, she was thought to be an "easy number." Everyone was trying to sell her something, or obtain something, or find favor with her. How could she turn this into a helpful experience? He said she was a teacher, by nature, as was seen from her experiences in the earth, and a natural magnet for the opposite sex as well as a great influence among her own sex. The Cayce source advised:

> Use these, then, as a means for telling of the love of Jesus. Let it become such an activity in self that everyone may come to know what would be the first words of the entity, and let them be this, though changed in form for the entity's own friends and experiences: Have you prayed to God today? Men won't follow you; men won't think you are an easy mark. Mean it, for in that manner ye may teach many a man with evil intents to know his place. For remember, no one, no one can stand in the presence of the Lord, the Christ, when words are thus spoken in earnest and in sincerity, no matter what their intent may be, and you will attract those with whom ye may administer much. 5089-2

The readings say that there is a physical expression that is beauty within itself if it is considered from that angle. When the mental and spiritual forces are guiding, then the outlet for this beauty becomes a normal expression of a normal healthy body.

A 34-year-old woman wondered about sexual relationships between husband and wife and asked: "Is it the correct understanding that this activity should be used only when companions seek to build a body for an incoming entity?" The answer:

Not necessarily. These depend, of course, on the individual concept of relationships and their activities. To be sure, if the activities are used in creative spiritual form, there is the less desire for carnal relationship; or, if there is the lack of use of constructive energies, then there is the desire for more of the carnal, physical reaction.   2072-16

A third person was told there should be agreement between two individuals in sexual relationships, and that only when there is such agreement should there be the relationship.

For the lack of such agreement brings more discordant notes between individuals than any portion of relationships with the opposite sex. The disagreements may be very slight at times, but they grow. For these relationships are the channels for the activity of creative forces and not by mere chance.   4082-1

Psychic Energy

When this energy is raised a notch, we may refer to it as psychic rather than sexual energy. It is the same energy in essence, but flows through a different circuitry. In Russia, Nelya Kulagina is able to move small objects without touching them. We were interested, of course, in the physiological changes during her demonstration of psychokinesis. We discovered that there were discernible and measurable bodily changes, such as a tremendous change in heart rate. We asked about her awareness of centers of energy in her body. She pointed specifically to the solar plexus area and her throat. The Russian scientists were so interested in the physical manifestations of energy that they could not be induced to talk about their connection to spiritual centers in the body. They saw such talk as naive physiology, rather than a key to understanding the phenomenon they were studying.

One of the most serious misconceptions about psychic energy is the notion that a direct relationship exists between a manifestation of psychic force and spirituality. For many, it still is not quite clear that the manifestation of the psychic is not necessarily spiritual. There is a group of religionists who say it is either of God or it is demonic. This extreme position is not instructive. We must rather begin to understand the circuitry, the physiology and the psychology of the motivation of these experiences.

The relationships between occult, psychic and mystical experiences can be very confusing. The Cayce readings discuss the differences among these terms. "Occult" is of the mind, directing the force with the mind, without consideration of spiritual or selfless purposes. "Psychic" is of the soul and relates to the purpose and intention of the soul. "Mystical" is the awareness and the experiencing of the Oneness.

The following reading, an apt example of the result of occult abuse, was given for a 44-year-old engineer with a diagnosis of epilepsy:

Here we have an emotional body well versed in the study of meditation, the study of transmission of thought, with the ability to control others.

Don't control others. Suppose thy God controlled thee without thy will? What would you become, or what would have been?   **3428-1**

He asked for the location in the physical body of the focal point of the epileptic attacks. (This is one of the few readings that mention specifically all seven centers and gives the position of the spine and the particular vertebrae related to the seven centers.) The reading makes it very clear that the misuse of the psychic force through the spiritual centers has led, in this specific case, to an extreme pathological manifestation—epilepsy.

Ours is a time in which there is a great deal of

discovery about the power of the mind. Sometimes this is termed "prosperity consciousness," sometimes "treasure mapping," and sometime just "prayer" or "positive thinking." But the application of this power is not always based on selfless purposes.

Dr. George Lamsa, translator of the Bible from the Aramaic language, tells this story of the time he first came to the United States. Some friends urged him to get an automobile. He always tried to make decisions like this through dreams, so he replied that he would seek guidance on this question. Within a week, he had received a check which would have enabled him to buy the automobile. Now, there is hardly a spiritually oriented one among us that would not have rejoiced and said, "See how wonderful God is and the way prayer and the law of abundance works! You express your need and there comes the money!" Well, Dr. Lamsa had received the check, but he had not received his guidance. About three weeks later he had a dream which was a very clear indication that getting an automobile at that time would hinder him in accomplishing the work he had to do. He sent the check back with a letter saying, "I think I drew this check to me because I wanted a car rather than because I was supposed to have it." Imagine a man with such character! The tricky thing about using the mind in this manner is that it works. The more it works, the more seriously we have to raise the question of what our purposes and motives are. Much of what is going on these days under the name "psychic" is, in Cayce's terms, occultism.

This mental energy can manifest in many forms, including healing. We still have a lot to learn about healing through the laying on of hands. Although this method of healing has a strong Biblical basis and encouragement from the Cayce material, it does not necessarily mean that all healing like this is spiritual.

In the laying on of hands, two parties are involved, the recipient and the channel. Let us look at the recipient of the healing energy to determine whether the healing is spiritual or occult. The determining factor is the purpose, why we want to be healed. Cayce

always asked people, "Why do you want to be healed?
So that you can be well enough to go back into the life
style that got you into the illness in the first place?"
Most of us want exactly that. We wish we could be well
so that we can return to the old pleasures. There is only
one valid motivation for wanting healing and that is a
commitment to change for the better in order to be of
greater service.

If we receive a healing, we ought to think of
ourselves as being in the eye of a cyclone. It was rough
before and it may get rougher afterwards! If we find
such a quiet period in our lives, it should be used in
every possible way to get ourselves on a more constructive path. This quiet period has an archetypal pattern in
the spiritual life clearly delineated in the Revelation of
John. It is symbolized by the four angels holding back
the winds from the earth. During such a period, we
have a reprieve for the purpose of changing. A thankful
attitude should be maintained for this very special
opportunity.

The other consideration in healing is the channel's
motivation and measure of attunement. The life force
may flow through channels who have varying degrees of
attunement. The consequent effects on the recipient
are, of course, potentially influenced by the channel's
attunement.

There are ways in which the one force may flow
through the channel and be directed outward to affect
physical objects. It may flow through an attuned system
of spiritual centers or it may come through an imbalanced
system. The kind of expression does not necessarily
indicate the motivation behind it. Psychokinesis may be
demonstrated; however, what is the purpose for it? For
different purposes, the energy flows through different
circuitries, giving consequently different effects both on
the channel and on the recipient.

Spiritual Energy

Now let us begin to examine the spiritual use of
the one force. A story about psychokinesis in the Old

Testament involves Elisha, the prophet (a psychic, according to the readings, second only to Jesus of Nazareth). A workman, laboring near a river, had borrowed an ax. While he was working, the ax head flew off the handle, sank into the river, and was lost. The workman was in distress. Along came Elisha who, out of a sense of concern for his fellow man, plunged a stick in the water, stirred it, and the ax head floated to the surface. The readings say that it was nothing to make the ax float. There are spiritual laws that can be discovered, developed and applied that would enable us to work with the force to manifest levitation. That is lawfulness. But the levitation was nothing. The desire to help another and the attunement enabling the would-be helper to be efficacious in the moment of need—that was something! But what if we apply that law without respect to purpose?

Let us apply this story of the floating ax-head analogously to the retrieval of information from the unconscious. If we have lived scores of times, the magnitude of our own unconscious records is immense. As we become interested in the concept of reincarnation, we may be prompted to seek recall of some of our past lives. The critical issue is: for what purpose? It is nothing to make the ax-head float (that is, it is nothing to retrieve information from the unconscious), but would you want everything recorded there to rise to the surface? Such memories may become stumbling blocks or stepping-stones according to timing and purpose. Optimally, distant memories would be sought only at a time and with respect to a purpose for which they would be made applicable in a helpful way. Otherwise, it might serve only to confuse.

I once attended a conference on healing to which many outstanding psychics and scientists were invited. Presentations were made on measuring the communication system between plants and human thoughts. Many of the psychics related accounts of their experiences, and some talked about the way in which plants respond to the energy field or "auras" of different individuals. They said they had seen how some plants would recoil from the auras of some people but reach out and draw energy from the auras of others. Then a clairvoyant shared an experience which I think is one of the funniest stories in the field of psychic perception. He was attending a service, in which an evangelical preacher was praying to the Spirit with great fervor saying, "Fill me, fill me, fill me!" To this man, the clairvoyant heard a voice reply, "I am filling you, but you leak!" The One Force is there ever flowing through us but what do we do with it is the question.

We have the challenge to use this force for a spiritual purpose. What do we mean by "spiritual"? Spiritual is related to motivation, intent, desire, and purpose; in other words, to an *ideal*. The setting of a spiritual ideal is our first step in making use of the life force in a spiritual way. Not only do the Cayce readings say that setting a spiritual ideal is the most important experience of any entity in the earth, but it is also a practical requirement for world peace. It is imperative for the people of the world to establish universally one ideal; it is the only basis for world peace. The readings indicate that it is going to happen, it must happen, sooner or later.

One of the exciting things in the Cayce material is the clarification of the relationship between the force and its manifestation with respect to ideals and patterns. There is an affinity between the One Force and an ideal which is consistent with it. In other words, if this One Force is love and we set the ideal as love, this will awaken and energize the pattern of love in our lives. There is an affinity of the power to the pattern. The power of love likes to flow through a pattern of love or a manifestation of love.

In the application of love, these steps need to be followed: (1) the setting of the ideal of love; (2) awakening it in meditation; and (3) application of it in our daily lives. In our use of the life force, there should be no condemnation of ourselves or of our activities. But we must change and grow. Rather than trying to stop doing wrong (resist not evil), let us start doing something right. If we will begin to apply this most fundamental psychological principle, great changes will begin to manifest in our lives.

To manifest this one force for spiritual purposes one of the clearest ways is in the life of prayer. Hugh Lynn Cayce once asked what would be the most important thing he could do for the work. He was told to get down on his knees and pray. Now, that is real work and one direct, selfless way to learn how to channel spiritual energy.

A common personal experience that all of us have had is the way in which, with a single thought, we can awaken different patterns of circuitry with the body. This cannot be emphasized too strongly or too often! The *mind*, the builder, chooses the circuitry in relation to the *ideal* we have set. A single thought can awaken the sexual response, a single thought can awaken the adrenal response of anger, resentment, hostility, jealousy, envy, and so on. Thoughts propelled by motivations have a mantric influence which bring them into manifestation. If sex, anger and jealousy illustrate response potentials, what would be other higher response potentials? Optimum circuitry involves the integration of the whole system at its optimum level. How may this be done?

In the Revelation, John has a vision of a book with seven seals. He cries because no one in heaven or earth is worthy to open those seals, but then the figure of the Christ in the form of a lamb comes and opens them. It is, then, the spirit of the Christ who can select that optimum circuitry, and not we ourselves at our lower level of consciousness. Rather than trying to pray open those powerhouses, those transformers of energy, we need to invite Him to open us in His wisdom through the pattern of Him resident within us, through the archetypal pattern of the Christ. Although we may talk theoretically about the one force, it is the setting of ideals, the practice of meditation and the application of these in the *personal experience* that will be most meaningful in working with this force.

Should we think of God as an impersonal force or

as a personal listening intelligence? Both, stated Cayce! In considering our use of the life force, let us work with the personal side for a moment. A few years ago, a Brother of the Order of St. Mary made a presentation on "The Love Life of a Modern Monk." He developed a beautiful story of the filial love of the Brothers for their spiritual mother, Mary. This was how the monks worked with the life force, in a creative and loving way, with a sense of a personal relationship to a spiritually pure and attuned being. As we consider this personal relationship, let us imagine ourselves as the Church, and therefore as the bride of Christ. The image of ourselves being the Church is one of the most challenging archetypal images in all of the spiritual teachings. It is the personal relationship with the Christ Spirit which enables us to work creatively, constructively and truly spiritually with the One Force. The multitude of desires that draw us in many directions must be refined and transformed to a greater love—and that is the love of the Christ.

The following Biblical quote sums up the considerations of our use of the life force:

> Though I speak with the tongues of men and of angels, and have not charity, I am become as a sounding brass, or a tinkling cymbal.
>
> And though I have the gift of prophecy, and understand all mysteries, and all knowledge; and though I have all faith, so that I could remove mountains, and have not charity, I am nothing.
>
> And though I bestow all my goods to feed the poor, and though I give my body to be burned, and have not charity, it profiteth me nothing.
>
> Charity suffereth long, and is kind; charity envieth not; charity vaunteth not itself, is not puffed up, doth not behave itself unseemly, seeketh not her own, is not easily provoked, thinketh no evil; rejoiceth not in iniq-

uity, but rejoiceth in the truth; beareth all things, believeth all things, hopeth all things, endureth all things. Charity never faileth: but whether there be prophecies, they shall fail; whether there be tongues, they shall cease; whether there be knowledge, it shall vanish away. For we know in part, and we prophesy in part. But when that which is perfect is come, then that which is in part shall be done away. When I was a child, I spake as a child, I thought as a child: but when I became a man, I put away childish things. For now we see through a glass, darkly; but then face to face: now I know in part; but then shall I know even as also I am known. And now abideth faith, hope, charity, these three; but the greatest of these is charity.   (I Cor. 13)

Gyroscope for the Spirit

The Edgar Cayce readings say that man, as a child of God, is a miniature replica of the universe. The pattern of the solar system is the pattern of the atom. Similarly, we are made in the image of God and are thus a miniature replica of the universe. There is nothing that man can observe in the universe that is not represented within us. We should look about us, both in nature—whether mineral or vegetable or animal—and in what we find in man's invention or discovery, for instructions regarding a better understanding of ourselves, our nature and our potential.

One of the most simple, yet fascinating and amazing of the discoveries or developments of man is the gyroscope. You have probably seen a toy gyroscope composed of an axle, a wheel, a flywheel and gimbals in which it revolves. It is a type of top. You wind it up with a string and pull it vigorously to turn the wheel very rapidly. It spins with remarkable stability. We are most interested in the applications of dynamic stability of the gyroscope to innumerable devices and vehicles. Is there within our own make-up something like the gyroscope which can give invariable direction and stability to our spirit?

In Paris, in 1852, a French scientist named Foucault took a long wire and a heavy weight which he suspended from a high ceiling. He let this pendulum swing and made a mark on the floor directly under the arc of the pendulum. As the audience watched, there grew a discrepancy that became larger and larger between the line of the arc in which the pendulum was swinging and the line he had drawn on the floor. The amazing thing indicated by the variance was not that the pendulum had changed but the floor due to the rotation of the earth. Regarding this, the encyclopedia Britannica states: "What was actually happening was, the pendulum was remaining *faithful* to its original arc with respect to space, but the earth, the floor of the exhibition hall, were moving under it due to the earth's rotation." This demonstration startled people in 1852 and it is still found exhibited in some major museums around the country.

Foucault coined the expression "gyroscope." "Gyro" means "rotation" and "scope" means "to see." This was a demonstration to see the rotation of the earth, or to paraphrase the Britannica's terminology, it was a demonstration to see the earth's lack of faithfulness. Yet, we measure nearly everything by criteria found in the earth for we consider it as being stable. When we talk about stability, we say, "Let's get down to earth." Yet the more we learn about the earth, the more we find there are problems in using it as a criterion of stability.

Within a few years, Foucault had developed a rotating wheel by which he could demonstrate the same principle; that was in the 1850s. In 1910, nearly 60 years later, a workable gyroscope was installed in a German warship to give it stability. Subsequently, there were developed huge gyroscopes, some weighing 600 tons, to keep ships stable in the waves. The great immense wheels revolved 900 revolutions a minute, keeping the ships stable. In 1925 the Japanese discovered that a small gyroscope could be used in directing fins which would keep the ship stable without the extra weight of the huge flywheels. It was the *principle*, then, applied and harnessed, that gave the ship its stability in the ocean waves, and not the weight of the wheel.

At the present time, we have gyroscopes in an array of devices and instruments. The uses of it are much more numerous than we might imagine. A modern marvel is all-weather flight. You have experienced this if you have flown in a modern jet. You have seen the amazing capability of airplanes to move in and through the clouds and to come down exactly where they want to be. We attribute this to navigational aids such as radar and ground controlled approaches, but what makes it safe for us to be up there at all is a gyroscope. The pilot depends upon an instrument that gives him an artificial horizon by which to fly the plane in the absence of visual contact with the ground. Although it is called the "artificial horizon," it is truer to the horizon than the airplane which is being tossed about and buffeted by the winds. That which enables the pilot to direct the plane unerringly with no other reference point and with such sureness that it never occurs to most airline passengers to question it, is the gyroscope.

As we consider stability of direction and purpose in our lives, we are reminded of the role of a balanced life style. To live a balanced, directed and stable life, we too need an inner gyroscope, especially a gyroscope of the spirit.

The Edgar Cayce readings challenge us to a lifestyle of balance. One of the needs for balance is between the inner and outer life. There is the external consciousness, the ego dealing with the things of the earth; there is the inner reality of the unconscious or the psyche, or the subconscious and superconscious, or the divine within. This concern of balance between the inner and outer may be characterized by the expression: "tune in and pour it out." These words are found almost verbatim in the Edgar Cayce readings, "tune in, pour it out." We can get off balance and talk only about the reasonable, rational, logical kind of thing to do; we can also get off balance as we turn about and turn within.

A military officer came to me saying he and his wife were very interested in the A.R.E., and they wanted to do the right thing. He said his wife had become very interested in dreams. She had found that if she slept until about 11 a.m., she had better dream recall. Then she found it took her all afternoon to record and analyze these dreams. The officer stated: "When I came home, she is still in her gown finishing her dream work." He added, "The worst thing about all this is that she's having a series of dreams about me having an affair with someone. That's not so, but she thinks these dreams are clairvoyant or precognitive." That was his story and complaint. In reflecting upon this story, it seems to me that it was she who was having the affair. She was having an affair with her own unconscious, and her dreams were showing this in a dramatic fashion.

Another form of imbalance that frequently develops with the approach to the inner life is in trying to contact the deceased. These attempts most frequently end in pain and sorrow. The Edgar Cayce readings say there are countless entities in the spirit plane who, not taking cognizance of their present state of affairs, still want to have a say in the affairs of the world. We expect those in the spirit plane to be wiser and more knowledgeable; but it just is not so. Merely because someone dies, does not mean that he has become other than a dead Methodist, a dead Catholic, or a dead Episcopalian, the readings say. As we orient toward the unconscious, we subject ourselves to an array of influences. Accuracy of information is not the criterion by which to evaluate these sources: sometimes there is a psychic quality, clairvoyant quality, a precognitive quality which may be accurate but not necessarily helpful.

Sometimes the voices tell you, "Now we are preparing you for a great work." You wake up in the middle of the night, your heart is beating, and they say, "We are rewiring you, so that you can handle all of this energy," and so it goes. Then they say, "We want you to do this, and we are testing you." Then you are required to begin to do ridiculous things. Some of what you get is beautiful and poetic; and if you ask, "Do you come from the Christ?" these voices may say "Yes." But soon you may find yourself on the street corner downtown at midnight waiting for their instructions, and then the voices begin laughing at you because they have been playing a joke on you, rather than preparing you for a great work.

A man came to Edgar Cayce after having gone to a

spiritualist where he had received a reading through an American Indian spirit guide named Running Horse. Running Horse told him he should marry a certain woman. He did marry her, but it did not work out very well. He asked Edgar Cayce why Running Horse had told him he should marry this woman. He was told that Running Horse had known both of them in a previous incarnation and was very interested in seeing the fireworks when the two got together.

Carl Jung said the unconscious makes a great servant, but a poor master. Before trying to reach the unconscious, we must establish an ability to cope with the external world. Yet there must also be that turning within to make the attunement for healing and that guidance that will help us cope.

Another type of balance with which we are concerned is the physical, mental, spiritual. Imagine a university with a chapel for spiritual work, a classroom for mental work, and a gymnasium for physical work. You may attend these workouts believing none of them has any relationship to the other. How many of us go to the gym to work out so we can meditate better in the chapel; and how many of us in the classroom expect to learn things that will help us both at the gym and in the chapel? As you can see, we may have these three dimensions represented without having them necessarily integrated.

As we mentioned in another chapter, in the East there is talk about different kinds of yoga: 1) Bhakti Yoga is devotion yoga (spiritual); 2: Jñana Yoga is knowing or cognitive (mental); 3) Karma Yoga is the application (physical). Sri Aurobindo's book, entitled *The Integration of Yoga*, deals with the integration of these three aspects. We also are working with an integrative exercise.

In a reading Edgar Cayce said that only when we have love, duty and reason together, do we have the beginning of an understanding of true love. Love represents Bhakti Yoga (spiritual); reason represents knowing or Jñana Yoga (mind); and duty represents Karma Yoga or the application or action (physical). Properly correlated we have then an integration of yoga as it relates to the physical, mental and spiritual applications.

Another form of balance found in the readings is the concept of cycles. Many do not like cycles. When it is summer, it is too hot and we wish it were cool. When it is winter, it is too cold and we wish it were warm. At midnight when we want to read further, or talk longer, or watch the late, late show, we wish the days were longer. Conversely in the morning when we do not want to get up, we wish the nights were longer. When we are youngsters, we wish we were older. When we are getting older, we wish we were young again. We don't like the idea of cycles in our lives. The concept of reincarnation, of course, deals on a much greater scale with cycles.

One of the things about cycles is the principle of proper timing, "in due season." We want things to bear fruit out of season and not in due season. Why was there cursing of the barren fig tree? When the Christ is there, *that* is due season. We want things to happen but not necessarily in God's timing or way. One of the things most clear about God's way of working in the earth plane is not only that He works in cycles and growth periods, but also that these cycles may stretch over considerable periods of time. In the *Earth Changes* and *Times of Crisis* readings, it is indicated that the heart of Christianity may move to China because the Chinese are willing to grow slowly. We fertilize something so it will bear fruit quickly without growing sound roots. The American way is to get production going quickly. We have difficulty with balance with respect to night and day, summer and winter, youth and age, and in working with the cycles of reincarnation.

According to the readings, the problematic or "down" periods in our lives are always growth oriented. Only because of God's love and work in our lives is there a growth. We must learn to love all cycles in our lives—whether up or down—since everything is a manifestation of the Divine. We need to learn to love the way He works, cyclically, and to appreciate what the winters and the nights are about as well what the summers and the days are about. One very beautiful aspect of cycles is that God allows us to meet ourselves over time in such dosages that we can manage. We do not have to meet the whole of ourselves all at once. This allows us to grow over an extended period of time.

The fourth type of balance is the middle path. When the Buddha started in his growth, he became an ascetic, an extremist, punishing his body, fasting and so on. When he moved away from extremes toward the middle path, his five original disciples were very disappointed, even though he made contact with that which gave him attainment. Jesus' way was the middle path also for which he received much criticism. He ate with the publicans and wine drinkers. He was not the ascetic John the Baptist was, and many people were disappointed. In John's latter days, he asked Jesus, "Are you He, or shall we look for another?" According to Edgar Cayce, John had grown up with Jesus, been initiated with Him, was preaching about Him and had said, "This man's sandal, I am not worthy to untie," and, "This is the one," when he saw the Spirit descend on Him. But he was expecting an extremist. The Pharisees sought someone who would follow more strictly to the law; the Essenes wanted someone who would withdraw into the hills; and the zealots wanted someone who would take action. It was a tremendous disappointment to them to have Jesus following the middle path.

One of the great weapons of the middle path is to have a sense of humor and the ability to see the ridiculous. Humor has a tremendous healing effect. In an analysis of humor, it is clear that a joke or something funny is the sudden seeing of the opposite of what we expect to see. As soon as we can say, "I see the other side," a tension is released and reconciliation can take place—that is what humor is all about. All of us feel there are two sides to a question until it comes to a question in which we are involved. Suddenly there is only one side—our side. The middle path sees both sides and humor is one of the great messengers of reconciliation.

These readings say Jesus laughed on the way to the cross. We have difficulty picturing this, but that is because we do not see that the other side of his defeat was jubilant victory for all of mankind. He knew the work He was doing; how could He do anything else but rejoice once that choice had been made?

At this point, it would be appropriate to stress again Carl Rogers' insight of creating an optimum environment for human growth. He had the faith that within man there was the ability to be healed. He saw that his job, as a counselor, was to provide an optimum environment. He articulated that environment to be "unconditional positive regard," and he taught that not only does the counselor need to have unconditional positive regard for the counselee, but that the individual must have unconditional positive regard for himself. This is an extremely difficult consideration, though a very sound one basically. The teaching, "resist not evil," indicates that the more we resist evil in ourselves, the more energy we give that thought form and the more we build it into ourselves.

Edgar Cayce gave a reading for an alcoholic who was told that in a previous life he had been a minister, a good man, who had preached against the demon rum. In this incarnation he was wrestling with a compulsion to drink simply because his dwelling upon the problem had built in a need to experience what it was like to deal with alcohol. This was for his own soul growth. Resisting not evil is a strange thing; for the readings say the vilest of the vile of the passions of man is just under the love of God. The vileness needs lifting, not attack.

The fifth approach to balance is the concept of being centered. Imagine someone walking a tightrope with a balancing rod and someone meditating in a lotus position. Which one is balanced? Both are. We think of balance as a precarious thing, but the balanced one truly is the one who is centered and stable. In Japan, they speak of a man who is centered as having *"hara,"* he has "belly." It is sensed that he moves from the center of his being and every action shows that. In Zen archery, you may spend weeks just shooting at a target two or three feet away. The criterion is not hitting the target, but rather getting centered.

Unfortunately, when we think about being centered and moving, we are likely to think goal instead of purpose. We think we are moving toward a goal. But "the way" is not "the way toward." "The way" is *how* we carry a quality of spirit into whatever we are doing. Regarding this challenge, we are told in the Biblical text to present our body as a living sacrifice as our reasonable service. When we have a choice, the only reasonable service is to choose rightly instead of wrongly. Even though the only reasonable thing is always to choose rightly, there is a subtler level at which we must learn to work. A criterion by which we can measure ourselves on whether we are on the spiritual path is when we start asking, "Is this the very best?" and not "Is it right or wrong?" If it is short of our standard, then it is less than reasonable.

The question is, how to keep centered. How does the gyro keep centered? There are two ingredients: it is launched, as it were, with respect to a direction, that is, it is given a commitment to which to be faithful; and it requires *energy* to keep it spinning. So: 1) direction or commitment; and 2) energy input. Or, as long as it is spinning, it tends to be faithful.

Let us apply these principles of dynamic stability to ourselves. The psalmist says, "Blessed is the man whose delight is in the Lord and in this law doth he meditate day and night. He shall be like a tree planted by the rivers of water that bringeth forth his fruit in due season, his leaf also shall not wither and whatsoever he doeth shall prosper." (Psalm 1) The beginning of this stability may be when we *direct* or commit the mind to the law of the Lord, because as Jesus said, "Heaven and earth may pass away, but my word will not." Think back to the gyroscope that is committed, even though the earth changes. Although the earth may change, and heaven and earth may pass away, He said, "My word will not pass away." Here is a dynamic stability of commitment. As the psalmist speaks of delighting day and night in the law, we see the giving of energy to that commitment.

Let us examine more fully what is meant by "... the law of the Lord." When we think about the law that is written in our hearts, minds and souls, is there not a relationship to the laws given in the Ten Commandments? Is there not a relationship of that law to the logos of the first chapter of John in which we are told that "In the beginning was the *Word*, the logos, and the Word was with God, and the Word was God, and everything that was made was made through the Word." As we pursue this understanding of the word of God as the law, we come to a better understanding of the *wisdom* in Proverbs, "When he appointed the foundations of the earth: Then I was by him as one brought up with him: and I was daily his delight... and my delights were with the sons of men." (Proverbs 8:29-31)

Are these attitudes not reminiscent of the Hebrews toward the Torah? Consider these words: image, wisdom, Torah, law, logos, the word, the mark (as in pressing on toward the mark). In the Cayce readings on meditation, we are told:

> If there has been set the mark (mark meaning here the image that is raised by the individual in its imaginative and impulse force) such that it takes the form of the ideal the individual is holding as its standard to be raised... then the individual (or the image) bears the mark of the Lamb, or the Christ, or the Holy One, or the Son, or any of the names we may have given to that which *enables* the individual to enter *through it* into the very presence of that which is the creative force from within itself—see?   281-13

This law, image, mark, or pattern is, in Jungian terms, the *archetype* of the Self. We may think of it as a thought-form or a quality of the mind, but it is also written into the body.

Let us consider more fully the meaning of the word "Torah." Torah means *the law*. It was applied to the first five books of the Old Testament, or such as the Ten Commandments. That was the law. Then somehow the Hebrew concept of Torah began to develop, embracing the whole doctrine, or the whole teaching. It grew to a theory that even before the world was made, there was the law, the Torah. The Jews expanded this concept and came to think of the Torah as a living creature. Finally, they arrived at a point of view that a single day devoted to the Torah outweighs a thousand sacrifices. Healing power was attributed to the Torah as a protection against suffering. Then it was taught that the Torah protects the whole world and in an attempt to do justice to this magnificent concept of the law, they concluded that, "God Himself studies the Torah."

When we say the Law, we must remember that the *law* is *love*—the law is love, love is law, God is love, God is law. The Old Testament teaches the "letter of the law" while the New Testament emphasizes the "spirit of the law" of love and grace. The apostolic writers thought of the Christ as a new Torah, a new law, but the quality of this law is love and life. It is not just the commandments or the words of Jesus or the Bible that is the new Torah. It is not the words given on Sinai or the Sermon on the Mount that is the new Torah, but rather the Christ Spirit.

This is not just the historical Jesus of the New Testament but rather the living Christ within us. It is not that Christ out there but that law written within our hearts and minds so that we can know and do it.

The Bible says the one thing Jesus had to learn was obedience. The Old Testament tells us a story about Abraham wanting a son. He was given a promise, "Your offspring will outnumber the stars of heaven." Moses wanted freedom. He was promised a "land of milk and honey." David wanted a kingdom, and Jesus—what did He want? To have eugenically perfect offspring? To establish a nation? To become king over the world? To build a temple where men could meet God? Just one thing—to do the Will of His Father! All He wanted to do was what He saw His Father doing, that one thing, obedience to the law, obedience to God, obedience to the Torah, to become the Torah, the Word, the law, one with God.

When Jesus became the Christ, He gave us through the examples of His obedience to the law and His devotion and total commitment to His ideal, the way or pattern for each of us to follow, that we too might become one with Him in the Father. The pattern is written in us; it need only be awakened by the ideal we set, our application of it in our daily lives and our reliance on the truth of His example. The readings recommend study of certain Biblical characters and passages as stimulants for arousing that pattern: for example, Moses and Joshua, the entire chapter of Deuteronomy 30, the 14th through 17th chapters of John, and of course the model of Jesus and His teachings.

As we attune to His Will through meditation and action, as we center on the Christ Spirit within to guide us in our every decision, we grow more deeply anchored to His Word, His law, His love. "Heaven and earth may pass away, but My Word shall not pass away." We will be with Him if we choose. In our coming times of crisis and testing, we can know the comfort of His ever present love and the wisdom of His ways.

If the Cayce prophecies are correct, it may get much worse before it gets better on this planet, of necessity. We may experience loss of family, job, health, home, happiness. We may find those things which we cherish most are those which must be removed, for we are to have no other things as objects of worship before Him. Stripped of what gives us security, we will be forced to find it in Him. His love for us would have it no other way, but that we turn back to Him. It is our choice of how and when. Let our love for Him be strong enough in return that we choose Him first, now.

Let us seek first the Christ Spirit to guide us to Him. He is our gyroscope, our stability, faithful not to the earth but to His original purpose. "The key should be making, compelling, inducing, having the mind one with that which is the ideal." (262-84) Let us set an ideal, set our gyroscope of the spirit spinning with commitment, and keep it spinning true by meditating on His law, reading His words, putting His will in action, seeking His presence both day and night. Commitment and faithfulness, these are the keys to a stability that will not pass.

Prescription for Times of Crisis

There is a great deal of talk about the times of crisis to come in the next 20 years. Not only do the Edgar Cayce readings make predictions about these times but prophesies are coming from other sensitives, from the churches, from fundamentalist groups, from Pentecostal groups, and from new-age groups. But the concern is not just from religious groups but also from unexpected sources. Geographers are talking about cataclysmic earth changes, economists are talking about recessions, and world specialists are talking about growing tensions in international political relations. There are wars and rumors of wars. When we think about times of crisis, we are likely to think of large-scale political, economic or even geological upheavals.

"Times of testing" was the term the Edgar Cayce readings used for these times. One of the characteristics of these times is the variety and diversity of the testing which we are undergoing individually. Each of us is being tested in a different and unique way. For some, the testing may be a challenge to one's health—whether it is poor health, pain or suffering. Others are being tested with an abundance of health, energy or unexpected resistance to disease. Some of us are being tested economically, by struggles and shortages, while still others are being tested with a surplus and affluence. Some of us are undergoing testing with the problem of loneliness, or of a life-confining companionship, of no companionship or of meaningful relationships. Others are undergoing tests by finding an abundance of friends, companionship, and loved ones. Some of us may be tested by actually undergoing cataclysmic changes in the earth affecting thousands about us; and some of us may be in safe areas but being tested in more individual ways.

When the readings speak of these times as times of testing, they do not necessarily give us clear-cut pictures of what the impact will be on all of us. According to this material, we have already been in this period of testing for 21 years—" '58 to '98." What has been going on in our lives in terms of testing? In order to discover what our test is, we need to look more deeply at the underlying nature of the test.

A series called the World Affairs Readings informs us more fully regarding these times (available in Circulating Files of A.R.E. members only and published in *Time of Crisis*). One of the readings is especially noteworthy. Let us examine it in full:

In the beginning when chaos existed in the creating of the earth, the Spirit of God moved over the face of same and out of chaos came the world—with its beauty in natural form, or in nature.

With man's advent into the world, then personalities, individualities, began to find expressions in *subduing* the earth, and man—with his natural bent—not only attempted to subdue the *earth*, but to subdue one another; and the result was the differences of opinions, the various sects, sets, classes and races.

As the earth was peopled, and the abilities of expansion were able to bring the various groups, or associations of groups or nations, they *could*—and *did*—withdraw into themselves, and build for themselves in the various portions of the world that known as the periods of advancement of some particular group of peoples.

As the world has advanced, all the various phases of man's developments have entered to make a different phase, either in the political, economic, or religious aspect of man's experience. In the various portions, then, of the world there has been builded those necessary developments for that particular group or portion of those peoples, or those developments of those peoples in their particular line.

With the advent of the closeness of the worlds coming into being, so that the man upon the other side of the world is as much the neighbor as the man next door, more and more have been the turmoils that have arisen in the attempt of individual leaders or groups to induce, force or compel, one portion of the world to think as the other, or the other group to dwell together as brethren with one bond of sympathy, or one standard for all.

With the present conditions, then, that exist—these have all come to that place in the development of the human family where there must be a reckoning, a one point upon which all may agree, that out of all of this turmoil that has arisen from the social life, racial differences, the outlook upon the relationship of man to the Creative Forces, or his God, and his relationships one with another, must come to some *common* basis upon which all *may* agree. You say at once, such a thing is impractical, impossible! What has caused the present conditions, not alone at home but abroad? It is that realization that was asked some thousands of years ago, "Where *is* thy brother? His blood *cries* to me from the ground!" and the other portion of the world has answered, *is* answering, "Am I my brother's keeper?" The world *as* a world—that makes for the disruption, for the discontent—has lost its ideal. Man may not have the same *idea*. Man—*all* men—may have the *same* IDEAL!

As the Spirit of God once moved to bring peace and harmony out of chaos, so *must* the Spirit move over the earth and magnify itself in the hearts, minds and *souls* of men to bring peace, harmony and understanding, that they may dwell together in a way that will bring that peace, that harmony, that can only come with all having the *one ideal;* not the one *idea,* but "Thou shalt love the Lord Thy God with all thine heart, thy neighbor *as* thyself!" This [is] the whole law, this [is] the whole answer to the world, to each and every soul. That is the answer to the world conditions as they exist today.

How shall this be brought about? As [they] each in their own respective sphere put into action that they know to be the fulfilling of that as has been from the beginning, so does the little leaven leaven the whole lump.

Man's answer to everything has been *Power*—Power of money, Power of position, Power of wealth, Power of this, that or the other. This has *never* been *God's* way, will never be God's way. Rather little by little, line upon line, here a little, there a little, each thinking rather of the other fellow, as that that has kept the world in the various ways of being intact—where there were ten, even, many a city, many a nation, has been kept from destruction. Though we may look upon, or feel that that which was given to Abraham—as he viewed the cities of the plain and pled for the saving of some—was an allegorical story, a beautiful tale to be told children—that it might bring fear into the hearts of those that would have their *own* way—may it not come into the hearts of those now, today, wilt *thou*, thine self, make of thine *own* heart an understanding that thou must answer for thine own brother, for thine own neighbor! and who is thine neighbor? He that lives next door, or he that lives on the other side of the world? He, rather, that is in *need* of understanding! He who has faltered; he who has fallen even by the way. *He* is thine neighbor, and thou must answer for him!   3976-8

The heart of the problem of these critical times is spiritual in nature. It relates to our relationship to God, but it is not a religious problem in the sense of awakening in ourselves religious loyalties and sentiments or of trying to find membership in an organization which will allay our anxiety. It is not even a matter of belief in God—that is taken for granted.

The Bible says we must *love* God. This is not an invitation but a commandment; it is a requirement and it must be done. Particularly in the Old Testament there are many extraordinary stories about the rise and fall of kingdoms. When we look at the lives of those leaders and kings, we find a vast array of sins for which the Lord is very forgiving. But there is one which is very serious—and that is idolatry. Because of narrow religious notions about what idolatry means, we have not understood the full impact of why this sin is so serious. It is not a question of religiosity but rather of the motivational basis of our lives.

What is really the source of all life? Where can we turn for a sense of security? What is the source of all our supply? What is the source of all our healing? What is the real source of any meaningful companionship? If the answers are not found in the living Spirit of God, then we are without hope.

When we discuss idolatry, we are considering specifically the question of where to put our trust—not in religious terms but in our everyday life. Do we trust in the stockmarket—is that the source of our security? If it wavers, do we waver? If our trust is in that on which the economy of the world rests, then we are like a cork bobbing on the ocean: every time there is a breeze, we wobble. This cannot possibly give us a sense of security or a stable source of supply. This cannot be our god.

Is our god in science or technology? For many years in teaching an introductory psychology class, I asked the students if they believed that science would eventually offer the solutions for the problems of mankind. For years, the answer was unanimously, "Yes." Suddenly in 1968-69, when I asked a class this very same question, I found only one person out of the whole class who said, "Yes"—and that was a retired colonel. The rest of the class, mostly 18-year-olds, said, "No," they did not think science was going to be the source of the answer to man's problems. So another god had failed! These young people had learned not to put their trust in science.

In the movie *2001: A Space Odyssey*, there was a computer named "HAL." He was a symbol of the technological god. It became very clear in that movie that the men had put their trust in HAL only to learn too late that he could not be trusted because of a fault in his programming. In the '30s, some put their trust in psychoanalysis, in the '50s and '60s it was small groups. In the mid-to-late '60s, it became social reform, but that did not work out either so it became political activism. Then there was Watergate and disillusionment. It became very clear that politics was not going to be the answer to our problems.

Where are we to turn? The answer is not to be found so much in an external solution to man's problems as it is in an *internal* one. Each of us should take an inventory in our own heart and mind of where we put our trust. Where do we have a sense that there is something secure; on what are we counting, on what are we banking? The test boils down to putting our trust in God. This test will take a different form for each of us. If we are counting on our retirement, Social Security, or investments, then that god is going to fail. If we are counting on medical science for our health, then we are going to be tested there, and that god is going to fail us. If we are counting on being a member of the right church, we are going to be tested there. And so each of us will be tested specifically in those places where we have placed our trust.

The year of 1910 was a time of testing for Edgar Cayce. He had been working with Dr. Ketchum, who had published an article in the *New England Medical Journal*. From that article came a lot of publicity from other newspaper articles, resulting in thousands of pieces of mail. To his surprise and dismay, Edgar Cayce found himself both famous and notorious.

Until fairly recently, the esoteric and metaphysical field was virtually unknown by the average individual. It was difficult for Cayce to understand how this gift might unfold as a life work which others could understand. He received an enormous amount of criticism and began to question whether or not his ability to give readings was a gift from God. He was all but ready to give it up. The only thing that persuaded him to remain.

in this field was a reading he had given for Uncle Ike that was so extraordinarily accurate that in following the advice given, his uncle was relieved of great pain.

Dr. Ketchum had written him a letter saying, "We'll set you up in your studio and give you what you need in order for you to give a couple of readings a day. This is going to be your life work." This was a time of testing; Edgar had to make a momentous decision. He sat in his room pondering this question, looking out at the stars all night long. As the morning dawned, he saw a Bible and waited until it was light enough to read. He went over to the Bible, looked at the opened page and saw that it was the 46th Psalm. That Psalm has been immortalized for all of us who have read *There Is a River*, the title of the Edgar Cayce story taken from this Psalm. This was his answer to his time of crisis. Upon reading that Psalm, with new faith, he wrote Dr. Ketchum, "We'll do it." At that major turning point, this Psalm became the basis for Edgar Cayce's answer to his life work. The 46th Psalm may very appropriately be called "The Times of Crisis Psalm." This "there is a river" psalm is also the "be still and know" psalm.

A man was told that in a previous experience he had been Achilles. He was head and shoulders above all other men—beautiful, powerful, a great leader. As Achilles, at about the age of 26, he was injured in battle by a sword blow to the heel. The readings say that this extraordinary entity, if he had learned to *be still* and quiet, could have healed the wound; but because he could not be still, gangrene developed and he died. It had been an extraordinary incarnation with extraordinary promise and opportunity ahead of him, but he could not *be still*. This story quickened my interest in the 46th Psalm which, to me, contains within it a prescription for these times. "God is our refuge and our strength." "Refuge" suggests a passive kind of retreat and "strength" suggests an active outgoing one. Yin and Yang. God is the masculine and the feminine force, the active and the passive. "God is our refuge and our strength, a very present help in trouble. Therefore, we will not fear." Now this is where the times of crisis come in which might refer to the prophesied earth changes and shifting of the poles: "Though the earth be removed, and the mountains be carried into the midst of the seas, though the waters thereof roar and be troubled, though the mountains shake with the swelling thereof, *there is a river* the streams whereof shall make glad the city of God. The holy place of the tabernacles of the most high."

"There is a river" is a more powerful Biblical analogy or parable than we may think at first. Psalm 1 begins saying that he who meditates day and night on the law of the Lord is like a tree planted by a river. Jesus said that He was the water of life and that he who partakes of this water, out of his belly would flow rivers of living water. Revelation 21-22 describes a beautiful ending, promising a new city and a glorious time. As you read of that promise, the culmination comes not with the symbology of these great structures alone but with there being a river in the heart of the city. "There is a river, the streams whereof shall make glad the city of God." It is one of the last and the most beautiful promises of the Revelation.

But, what does that mean? There is an access to the Spirit that is the immediate source of life, light, love and healing. "There is a river the streams whereof shall make glad the city of God, the holy place of the tabernacles of the most high. God is in the midst of her, she shall not be moved. God shall help her and that right early." Now more times of crisis scriptures: "The heathens raged, the kingdoms were moved, He uttered His voice, the earth melted. The Lord of Hosts is with us, the God of Jacob is our refuge. Come, behold the works of the Lord, what desolations He has made in the earth. He makes wars to cease unto the end of the earth, He breaks the bow and cuts the spear asunder, He burns the chariot in the fire." And now here is the prescription: "Be still and know that I am God. I will be exalted upon the heathen, I will be exalted in the earth. The Lord of Hosts is with us. The God of Jacob is our refuge."

In the midst of earth changes, wars, turmoils and

all manner of frightening things here is an invitation to *be still*. Achilles was not able to do it and we all seem to have a difficulty doing it. We are so anxious about external concerns that we are suspicious of meditation. Anyone talking about meditation becomes suspect of retreating from the real world and of being impractical.

When we read the Cayce readings on prophecies of earth changes, such as the possible inundation of California, we think we can pray and change that prophecy. Should not we rather say, "Let that be in the Lord's hands. He knows that of which we are in need." It may truly be said that there are some things we need to meet in the right spirit and in the silence, rather than in trying to change a situation or to do something to prevent a change from occurring. A typical American attitude toward an undesirable situation is "Let's do something about it!" But remember the beautiful Serenity Prayer in which we ask: "God grant me the serenity to accept the things I cannot change, courage to change the things I can, and wisdom to know the difference." We are not very good at accepting things that cannot be changed. Although we may like this prayer, we may not be inclined to accept the notion that some things cannot be changed. Accepting this concept is not the American way. A psychiatrist from Mexico conducting objective research at the University of Texas a few years ago found that Americans had healthier attitudes about things that could be changed, but Mexicans had healthier attitudes about things that could not be changed—such as the death of a loved one. He found that even in such relatively irreversible circumstances, Americans were futilely trying to do something about the situation—such as giving expensive funerals. We must be very discriminating in our opinions on what needs to be changed. As we learn to be still, our ability to discriminate is sharpened.

When we consider the prophecies of changes in these times of crisis, we are likely to say, "What do we do about it?" The instruction given us in this particular psalm of crisis is: "Be still and know."

It all boils down to this question, "In what or in

whom do we put our trust?" Do we put our trust in our ability to manipulate things, or do we put our trust in God, knowing that there is only One Force at work in the universe, knowing it is a good force, and knowing that it is working for good in the lives of us all.

In the face of the array of challenges which we as individuals, as a group, as a nation, are going to meet, there is going to be extraordinary fear, anxiety, panic and hysteria unless we have learned to practice the stillness. We have yet a little time to practice, but we do not know for how long. Perhaps we have a year or two or three in which to be free of pain, or free of economic challenge, or free of earth changes. We have a little time to get ourselves centered, to start practicing meditation and to start practicing the awareness of His presence. Let us not wait until the crisis is upon us; let us not wait until the physical pain becomes unbearable; let us not wait until the economic pressure makes us so hungry that it is not comfortable to meditate; let us not wait until the economic or energy shortage is such that the winters are too cold for us to be comfortable in our practice of the silence. Let us establish a centering now by being still and quiet through the practice of meditation so that when the tests are more painful and the pressure is stronger, we will know how more surely to find that quiet place.

Why be still? There is no knowing of God outside of His manifesting in our own inner awareness. The spiritual quest is not like a mountain with many paths up to the top; there is only *one* way to God—and that is through meeting the Spirit within our own inner self. The Divine must be manifested in the consciousness and then applied in the life of the individual. There is only one way: it is God or call it by whatever name— the Divine, the Living Spirit flowing through us in our lives, our consciousness and, most importantly, in our application.

Meditation properly applied is exactly that! Meditation is practicing awareness of the Presence. Meditation is practicing awareness of the flow of the Spirit through us. The prescription for times of crisis is to *be still* and know God. We can begin to work on this through the practice of meditation. Let us discuss some essential points regarding meditation. It is not meditation that does the work, nor a meditation technique that is the proper approach to God, but it is the Living Spirit working through us that effects the changes. Do not depend on meditation, depend upon God. Do not get caught up in worrying about the process of meditation; concern yourself rather with the awareness of Him by inviting and experiencing His presence.

Someone asked Edgar Cayce, "Are my meditations bringing results?" And the answer was, "Keep that consciousness that in Him all things are done well." (281-4) Cayce shifted the emphasis away from the proper technique of meditation to the sense of the confidence of the power of God to effect change in our lives.

Another point: *The Secret of the Golden Flower* says, "All holy men have bequeathed this one to another: all methods end in silence." We know historically that Christian meditators, Buddhist meditators, Hindu meditators, and Sufi meditators, have all had glorious and life-transforming experiences. In our attempts to be broad-minded and generous to the position of the other fellow, we may come to a notion that it does not matter how we practice meditation. One technique is as good as another; what is important is just that we meditate. I am not so sure of this! It is only by going to the very heart of these teachings that we may find the Oneness. They are not all the same at the superficial level. So I do not think all the approaches to meditation are of the same value.

This leads us to a consideration of the importance of motivation. We have stressed time and again the importance of the ideal. But we have talked so much about writing down the ideals that we may get a sense that the ideal is something *out there* on a piece of paper instead of the living quality of spirit going on within us. It is hoped that by putting our ideals on paper, we can take a major step toward awakening the highest spirit within us. We have the potential within us for manifold motivations; but it is the motivation of love that selects the circuitry, if our bodies are to be as instruments through which the One Force may flow. The selection of that circuitry affects not only the experience we may have but also what we may manifest in our lives! And so the setting of the motivation, the awakening of the motivation, is of the utmost importance in meditation.

At the beginning of our discussion, we talked about the readings which say that the whole world must come to have the same ideal. The desire, the motivation, the driving spirit behind the meditation must be the high ideal.

A man who received a life reading was told he had an American Indian incarnation with the name of Tecumseh. He had been a trader, facilitating commerce between the white men and the Indians. Through that work, he had done a service to both groups, the white man and the Indian. He had also been an astute businessman and in the process had accumulated a considerable fortune which he had buried near a river in Alabama. In this present incarnation he was told that because he had a high motivation in that experience as Tecumseh, the money was properly his, and he could find it and take it. All he had to do was to go there, meditate and reawaken that quality of motivation by which he had come by that wealth, and then he would remember where he had buried it.

This indeed was a time of crisis for him. He was facing a test. He went there, but he was so excited about locating the money that he could not be still and quiet. He could not remember. As we read the correspondence between him and Edgar Cayce, we find disillusionment, disappointment, and anger. He felt that the readings could tell him where the treasure was located if they would. Why did they not just go ahead? They had brought him this far, why did they not tell him where to dig?

The point is that the wealth belonged to him only with respect to the motivation by which he had achieved it. It was his only insofar as he was able to awaken the spirit of selfless service. It is as though the record of the memory of the burial place was contained within the motivation of service. Most of us are probably wealthy with a number of talents in just the same manner. Our remembrance of them would unfold following the awakening of the motivations which led to their development.

It is not some whimsical thing with God. It is simply that a circuitry exists within us for attuning to the universe, and the selector of that circuitry is mind and motivation. Angry words select the circuitry of the adrenals, sexual fantasies select the circuitry that puts us in attunement with the universe. Attunement is not whimsical, but rather lawful. In our motivations the establishment of the ideal of selflessness, not only on paper but in the glands of our bodies, is an essential part of meditation.

Another essential of meditation relates to the principle from the readings and other sources that mind is the builder. The mind is always involved in meditation, for there is no such thing as a blank mind. Mind, as the builder, is at work in everyday meditations as well as in deep meditation. Therefore, in a certain sense, meditation is going on 24 hours a day—whether it is in dreaming sleep, non-dreaming sleep or during the day. The mind is working all the time; it is building what we supply to our bodies and what we are preparing for our souls. Meditation is a very special case of mind as the builder because when we are still and quiet, there is more energy and more transformation.

Meditation, as it builds, is a memorization process. The emotions, motivations and experiences dwelt upon in that state are more deeply "memorized." What we think, we become; what we think during meditation, we become more surely. The thoughts being held during an hour of meditation affect us differently in quantity, but not in quality, from those being held in any hour during the rest of the day. In this hour, we establish a direction for the mind and retain the awareness of His presence, then during the rest of the day we may remain centered in our awareness of God.

What we do with the mind is of special significance in the outcome of meditation. The essential consideration is the relationship between the practice of meditation and the desired results. Many people try to meditate; but because they do not have beautiful experiences, they think their efforts are in vain. No effort in meditation is in vain. But what is the criterion by which we should measure our meditation? Is it not the changed life?

Something very interesting, but misleading, occurred a few years ago with the growing use of drugs and the countermovement to it with the wave of interest in meditation. A few years ago, you may have heard people say, "I don't have to take drugs now, I can get high on meditation." That assertion missed the whole point of meditation. Many people think that we meditate to have an experience, but the true purpose for meditation is to enhance the quality and direction of our soul's growth in our everyday lives.

The Secret of the Golden Flower asserts, "If you only meditate for a quarter of an hour, by it you can do away with the ten thousand aeons and a thousand births. All methods end in quietness. This marvelous magic cannot be fathomed." (p. 33) And in another place it states, "One must not content oneself with small demands but must rise to the thought that all living creatures have to be redeemed." (p. 8) Hence, we should not be content just to have a "high" experience during those 15-20 minutes, but we should measure our meditation by the changes occurring in our lives throughout the months and years. The real working quality of meditation is the transformation that takes place at an unconscious level. It is not ego fantasies for a few minutes of "high" experiences. "Within our six-foot body, we must strive for the form which existed before the laying down of heaven and earth. If today people sit and meditate only one or two hours, looking only at their own egos, and call this reflection, how can anything come of it?" (p. 34)

The readings state that there is not a question we can ask that cannot be answered from within when we are in attunement. Many people who came to Cayce asked: "What about this?" "What about that?" "What about the other?" In almost every case in responding to these questions, Cayce stated, "This may best be answered from within," and he instructed them on how to make that attunement in order to receive the answer. Yet, even though we can do this, we still seek outside help as did one person who asked, "Where can I get concrete guidance besides from the inner voice?" It seems easier to go without for answers.

Another asked if he could receive guidance from meditation. The reply was, "On any subject! whether you are going digging for fishing worms or playing a concerto!" (1861-12) The answer to every question, every problem is *within;* there is no question too great or too small to bring to the throne within. It is a promise of which we may be sure! Many people have a tremendous resistance to working with this procedure of attunement for decision making. Basically, we would rather decide "on our own" than to have even our own higher inner voice direct us.

The readings inform us that through pain, suffering and disillusionment, we will eventually learn that our will really is the same as God's will and that His will for us is really our best choice. The conscious mind is convinced that it is the final arbiter and the source of our creativity. This aspect of the mind is always misleading us with its reason, intellect and bias.

During meditation, there must be a quality of fearlessness, since fear and meditation are incompatible. One exceptional case history in the readings' files describes a woman whose illness developed through every major organ in her body, with each step in the pathological process being a result of a combination of anxiety about meditation and the practice of it. Her whole body—glandular system, autonomic nervous system, central nervous system, liver, kidneys, heart, and intestines—got involved in that pathological process, making us realize that the only thing we have to fear is fear itself. Anxiety, doubt, and fear—these are always more destructive than any original problem. Fear always does us in!

Some worry about the dangers of meditation, but let us say that the only thing more dangerous than

meditating is *not* meditating. The only safe place is
when we are practicing an awareness of His presence.
At every turn of doubt we must respond immediately,
"Be not afraid, it is I," knowing that the *I* is His
promise, "Lo, I am with you always." (Matthew 28:20)
We can apply this awareness to every challenge in our
lives. Every challenge can become either a stumbling
block or a stepping-stone. If we sense that the challenge
is an opportunity for soul growth, then we can see the
Divine working in our lives and with assurance feel,
"Be not afraid, it is I," since it is He who presents
Himself to us in that opportunity. If we do not have this
attitude, then each experience becomes a stumbling
block.

Another form of this principle is found in the
saying, "When the student is ready, the teacher will
appear." Many believe this statement refers to the
appearance of a guru, a living master. However, it may
also refer to an attitude about life. When we are ready
to be a student, then everything can be met as a
learning experience. Therefore, when we are ready to
learn, whatever we are meeting or experiencing can
become a stepping-stone instead of a stumbling stone.
Being able to accept everything as a stepping-stone is
part of believing and trusting in God with confidence
that He knows what He is doing.

Finally, as an essential of meditation, there should
be a continuing examination, inventory and evaluation
in our lives with that which the readings suggest to be
the most important question that anyone can ever ask,
"What will I do with the man called Jesus?" Ours is a
time where there is a broadening and an opening up of
attitudes dealing with religious questions.

The readings in their universal quality speak of the
brotherhood of all men. They see God as operative in
every person because we are all spiritual beings. They
state that no soul is incarnate in the earth who has not
had an experience or quickening related to the awareness
of the one God. All other souls have been eliminated
from incarnating at this time. Every soul in the earth
has not only heard, "the Lord thy God is One," but has

also a special quality that would draw him in the direction of the Spirit. We should be able to look at every individual in a new light, knowing that all who are incarnate in the earth today have something special within them related to the seeking to be one with God. We have a very special opportunity now to learn and experience more deeply the true meaning of the life and work of Jesus of Nazareth.

In these and the coming difficult "times of testing," we must practice this prescription: Be still and know that I am God. Then we may have the awareness of His Presence, His friendship, His fellowship, and we may claim His promises that He will not leave us comfortless, that He is with us always, and that "He which hath begun a good work in you will perform it until the day of Jesus Christ." (Philippians 1:6)

> God is our refuge and our strength, a very present help in trouble. Therefore will not we fear, though the earth be removed, and though the mountains be carried into the midst of the sea; Though the waters thereof roar and be troubled, though the mountains shake with the swelling thereof. Selah. There is a river, the streams whereof shall make glad the city of God, the holy place of the tabernacles of the most High. God is in the midst of her; she shall not be moved: God shall help her, and that right early. The heathen raged, the kingdoms were moved: he uttered his voice, the earth melted. The Lord of hosts is with us; the God of Jacob is our refuge. Selah. Come, behold the works of the Lord, what desolations he hath made in the earth. He maketh wars to cease unto the end of the earth; he breaketh the bow, and cutteth the spear in sunder; he burneth the chariot in the fire. Be still, and know that I am God: I will be exalted among the heathen, I will be exalted in the earth. The Lord of hosts is with us; the God of Jacob is our refuge. Selah.   Psalm 46

THE EDGAR CAYCE LEGACIES

Among the vast resources which have grown out of the late Edgar Cayce's work are:

The Readings: Available for examination and study at the Association for Research and Enlightenment, Inc. (A.R.E.®) at Virginia Beach, Va., are 14,256 readings consisting of 49,135 pages of verbatim psychic material plus related correspondence. The readings are the clairvoyant discourses given by Cayce while he was in a self-induced hypnotic sleepstate. These discourses were recorded in shorthand and then typed. Copious indexing and cross-indexing make the readings readily accessible for study.

Research and Information: Medical information which flowed through Cayce is being researched and applied by the research divisions of the Edgar Cayce Foundation. Work is also being done with dreams and other aspects of ESP. Much information is disseminated through the A.R.E. Press publications, *A.R.E. News* and *The A.R.E. Journal.* Coordination of a nationwide program of lectures and conferences is in the hands of the Department of Education. A library specializing in psychic literature is available to the public with books on loan to members. An extensive tape library has A.R.E. lectures available for purchase. Resource material has been made available for authors, resulting in the publication of scores of books, booklets and other material.

A.R.E. Study Groups: The Edgar Cayce material is most valuable when worked with in an A.R.E. Study

Group, the test for which is *A Search for God*, Books I and II. These books are the outcome of eleven years of work by Edgar Cayce with the first A.R.E. group and represent the distillation of wisdom which flowed through him in the trance condition. Hundreds of A.R.E. groups flourish throughout the United States and other countries. Their primary purpose is to assist the members to know their relationship to their Creator and to become channels of love and service to others. The groups are nondenominational and avoid ritual and dogma. There are no dues or fees required to join a group although contributions may be accepted.

Membership: A.R.E. has an open-membership policy which offers attractive benefits.

For more information write A.R.E., Box 595, Virginia Beach, Va. 23451. To obtain information about publications, please direct your query to A.R.E. Press. To obtain information about joining or perhaps starting an A.R.E. Study Group, please direct your letter to the Study Group Department.

ABOUT THE AUTHOR

HERBERT BRUCE PURYEAR is a clinical psychologist who has specialized in integrating the insights of psychical research, depth psychology and comparative religion. This study has included an emphasis on a study of the archetypal symbolism of dreams and of religious, mystical and psychical experiences. He has also made an intensive study of the psychic readings of Edgar Cayce.

He is the author of a number of articles and several books including *The Edgar Cayce Primer*, *Reflections on the Path*, and *Sex and the Spiritual Path*, and is co-author of *Meditation and the Mind of Man*.

Dr. Puryear is currently President of Logos World University which is dedicated to research and training in the integration of the fields of psychic research, comparative religions and holistic healing.

The Edgar Cayce story is one of the most compelling in inspirational literature. Over the course of forty years, "The Sleeping Prophet" would close his eyes, and enter an altered state of consciousness, and then speak to the very heart and spirit of mankind on subjects such as health, healing, dreams, meditation, and reincarnation. His more than 14,000 readings are preserved at the Association for Research and Enlightenment.

Bantam has an entire library of books on Edgar Cayce. See if your bookshelf isn't missing one.

EXPLORE THE SPIRITUAL WORLD WITH SHIRLEY MACLAINE AND JESS STERN

Check to see which of these fine titles are missing from your bookshelf:

Titles by Jess Stern:

☐ 23830-2	EDGAR CAYCE: SLEEPING PROPHET	$3.95
☐ 25150-3	SOULMATES	$3.95
☐ 05075-3	SOULMATES, a Bantam hardcover	$14.95
☐ 24082-X	YOGA, YOUTH, AND REINCARNATION	$3.50

Titles by Shirley Maclaine:

☐ 05094-X	DANCING IN THE LIGHT, a Bantam hardcover	$17.95
☐ 05035-4	OUT ON A LIMB, a Bantam hardcover	$15.95
☐ 25045-0	OUT ON A LIMB	$4.50
☐ 25234-8	"DON'T FALL OFF THE MOUNTAIN"	$4.50

Look for them in your bookstore or use the coupon below:

Special Offer
Buy a Bantam Book
for only 50¢.

Now you can have an up-to-date listing of Bantam's hundreds of titles plus take advantage of our unique and exciting bonus book offer. A special offer which gives you the opportunity to purchase a Bantam book for only 50¢. Here's how!

By ordering any five books at the regular price per order, you can also choose any other single book listed (up to a $4.95 value) for just 50¢. Some restrictions do apply, but for further details why not send for Bantam's listing of titles today!

Just send us your name and address and we will send you a catalog!